Y0-BDV-399

THE THRESHOLD
(*Umbartha*)

A
Classic
Collection

For those who value taste.

JABBAR PATEL'S

THE THRESHOLD

(Umbartha)

Screenplay by
VIJAY TENDULKAR

Script reconstructed and translated by
SHAMPA BANERJEE

SEAGULL BOOKS
CALCUTTA 1985

SEAGULL BOOKS
A Publishing Programme for the
arts and media scene in India

© Seagull Books Calcutta 1985

Cover design by Ashit Paul

ISBN 0 86132 096 4

*Published by Naveen Kishore, Seagull Books
26 Circus Avenue, Calcutta 700 017*

*Printed in India by P. K. Ghosh at Eastend Printers
3 Dr Suresh Sarkar Road, Calcutta 700 014*

*Blocks engraved and cover printed by
Reproduction Syndicate, 7-1 Bidhan Sarani,
Calcutta 700 006*

Introduction

Umbartha is not one of those films likely to inspire or figure in an intellectual or academic discussion. I doubt if it was ever so designed. On the contrary, its significance lies in the fact that it strikes a rare balance between a serious theme honestly presented and a framework that holds the interest of the motley crowd that usually throng the urban cinemas. It also presents an unusually uncompromising view of the intelligent and aware urban woman who has so far existed almost entirely outside the silver screen, surviving in an atmosphere vitiated by the common images of women that are perpetuated by the commercial cinema.

In a country where the politics of corruption has penetrated deep into the social soil, creating moral norms that are inherently false and immoral, women like Sulbha continue to fight their battles alone. Their struggle is made more acute by the fact that the real enemies hide behind a facade of justice and truth, social respectability and moral self-righteousness. The blacks and whites exist more in fiction than in reality. Danger stems more from men like Subhash, who is ostensibly honest and rational, rather than from a patently corrupt politician like Bane. It is ultimately men like Subhash, with their knowledge of all the loopholes in the legal system, who help to keep the Banes of this world alive and free.

In her spacious, comfortable bungalow, suggestive of a generous life-style, Sulbha's dilemma could easily be typical of what is faced by any idle rich woman who wants to project herself outside her home, where she has nothing to do, as a socially useful and important person. That it does not happen to be so is because, in effect, in her own home Sulbha plays the role of the underprivileged. She is not allowed to look after or discipline her own daughter because there is ostensibly an emotional justification why Maya, the childless sister-in-law, should be the person in charge of the child as well as the household. The grim, authoritarian mother-in-law expects Sulbha to help in her own field of social work, irrespective of the fact that Sulbha has been trained in a different field and has other aspirations. Sulbha also reacts strongly against the value system that operates at her own level of society where the whole family, including her stern mother-in-law, find nothing immoral in Subhash's legal prevarications by means of which he plans to victimize a poor and wronged woman in order to save the reputation of an established member of the medical profession who has money and power at his command. Sulbha, a silent spectator, already finds herself an outsider in her own world.

At one level, the Mahilashram, where Sulbha goes to work, becomes a microcosm of the outside world. Administrative authoritarianism rules the lives of a group of deprived women who are virtually imprisoned behind its walls. In the outside world these women have been exploited by the same class of men that have helped to put them in the Mahilashram—the garbage dump which helps to keep society clean. In the prison-like atmosphere of the Mahilashram, any rebelliousness is ruthlessly suppressed. The managing committee, made up of leaders of society, have neither the time nor any real concern for the problems of these women. Instead, they find it convenient to overlook the corrupt way in which the home has been run so far.

It is not just because Sulbha honestly attempts to understand their problems that she is finally accepted by the women in the home. It is also because her own involvement with her work alienates her husband, and she soon finds herself unconsciously moving towards the same lonely world that these women share in the Mahilashram. Paradoxically, however, even in this isolated and neglected corner, the false moral codes of the outside world hold sway. The lesbian relationship of Jangam and Sunanda, born directly out of this isolation, brings to a head the latent frustrations of the inmates, who demand the removal of the two girls from the home. The reason they give is the same as that which society puts forward to justify their segregation. They are unclean. Tirodkar, the reputed journalist who is a member of the managing committee, decides to use the story as a scoop. The Chairperson, highly indignant about the moral implications of the incident, holds it up as an example of the many indiscretions committed by Sulbha, who had been openly fighting against removing the two girls from the home.

And then Bakula and Gulab run away from the Mahilashram. Bred in the slums of a big city, they find this the only way to reach out towards freedom again. When the police bring them back, they are driven by their feelings of utter defiance and resentment to set themselves on fire.

Charges of gross mismanagement are brought against Sulbha. Facing a smug and seemingly cold and disinterested listener—the one-man commission, Sulbha speaks out at last. Her bitterness and anger at the self-righteous callousness of the world outside is lost on the man on the other side of the table. He remains unmoved, a little sarcastic, and somewhat amused by Sulbha's passionate appeal. The charges are not proved and Sulbha resigns. But when she comes back home, unknown to her, her life has turned a full circle, and the rejection of Sulbha is complete. Her daughter refuses to respond to her, and at night, after making love to her dutifully, Subhash explains that he has taken a mistress. Sulbha, he assures her, will retain all her rights as his wife. Her position in the home will remain as before, her prestige will not suffer. But she must make allowance for his needs just as he has endeavoured to understand hers.

Sulbha has finally joined the ranks of the women she had set out to save. She chooses freedom, however, and leaves her home for an unknown destination.

In our own lives we very often fail to recognize the exploitative nature inherent in our relationships. To all appearances, Subhash is a good husband. He is emancipated: he allows his wife to leave home to take up a job. He is honest: he admits that he has taken a mistress when he could easily have kept quiet. He hopes she will understand and reconcile herself to the new situation. From his point of view he feels he has done nothing wrong. When Sulbha had been staying at home, she had made her silent compromises. But now, with her new-found knowledge and awareness, she takes stock of her world, once more silently, and decides that she must leave it behind. She crosses the threshold and enters the larger world outside alone, armed only with her determination not to accept defeat.

Umbartha is a film for the many Sulbhas of this world who have not yet crossed the threshold.

SHAMPA BANERJEE

A Note on the Text

This script is based on a shot-by-shot viewing of the film. Mr P. K. Nair, Director, National Film Archive of India, was kind enough to provide a print of the film and the required facilities for the viewing. Aditi Kanitkar transcribed the dialogues and Shaila Prabhu helped with the translation. Jabbar Patel revised the text before publication.

Credits

Direction   Jabbar Patel

Script and dialogue   Vijay Tendulkar

Story   Based on the novel *Beghar* by Shanta Nisal

Camera   Rajan Kinagi

Art Direction   Dinanath Chauhan

Editing   N. S. Vaidya

Music   Hridaynath Mangeshkar

Lyrics   Vasant Bapat, Suresh Bhatt

Sound   Ravindra Sathe

Produced by   D. V. Rao, Jabbar Patel

Marathi / 135 minutes / Eastmancolor / 35 mm / 1982

Also in Hindi version, as *Subah*

Cast

Artistes	*Characters*
Smita Patil	Sulbha
Girish Karnad	Subhash
Shrikant Moghe	Mohan
Ashalata	Maya
Kusum Kulkarni	Nani
Purnima Ganu	Rani
Daya Dongre	Sheila Samson
Shriram Ranade	Tirodkar
Satish Alekar	Vadimbe
Manorama Wagle	Kamlabai
Chanchal Suryavanshi	Gulab
Aruna Vigar Dive	Bakula
Nandini Chavre	Mangala
Swarupa Khopkar	Utpala
Rani Sabnis	Subhadra
Sandhya Kale	Sunanda
Sushma Deshpande	Jangam
Manik Bhandare	Jaswandi
Jaimala Kale	Sugandha
Sushila Vansale	Champa
Surekha Divekar	Farida
Sujal Vatve	The mad girl
Subhash Godbole	One-man commission

The credits in reverse on a black background.

Subhash's home. An old style bungalow on spacious grounds with a lawn in front of the house, fringed with tall trees. Sulbha sits alone on a cane chair in the middle of the lawn.

The flowers in the garden around the lawn.

Music begins on a closer view of Sulbha's profile. Camera moves to the left slowly, till it faces her. She is staring in front of her thoughtfully.

The palm trees that fringe the lawn.

Another view of Sulbha. She leans back on the chair and looks up, still pensive.

Subhash's mother comes out to the porch where the car stands waiting for her. Her sons and their wives call her Nani, a term of endearment, instead of the more usual Aai, which stands for Mother in Marathi. With her is her secretary, Deshpande, and her elder son Mohan's wife, Maya. She talks as they walk up to the car.

NANI: I've yet to get the accounts of the Harijan Ashram, Deshpande.

DESHPANDE: I'll have them ready for you within a day or two.

NANI: And what about the vacancy for a technician in the Blood Bank?

DESHPANDE: I shall see to it.

NANI: Oh yes, and I have also spoken to the Minister this morning over the telephone about the institution for the handicapped. (*She enters the car.*)

DESHPANDE: That is good.

Sulbha sits in the lawn, absent-mindedly toying with her glasses. Her mother-in-law and Maya can be heard talking in the background.

MAYA (*off*): Should I send you your lunch today, Nani?

NANI (*off*): No, I'll make some arrangement for myself today. Send Rani her lunch.

Maya stands near the car.

MAYA: Yes, I shall.

The car moves away down the driveway. In the distance Sulbha is seen sitting with her back to the camera. Maya goes right, and out of the frame. The camera closes in on Sulbha, who rises from her chair and starts moving away.

Sulbha moving among the trees of the garden. The camera moves with her to the left. She stops with her back to the camera, looks around, then starts moving again.

Sulbha walks past a flowering bush, with the porch in the background. The camera moves with her as she walks to the entrance of Mohan's nursing home. Mohan is heard talking to a patient.

PATIENT (*off*): But Doctor, the fever has still not come down.

MOHAN (*off*): You mustn't worry. (*Mohan comes into view, walking towards Sulbha.*) It's my responsibility. Just don't worry. (*He stops to talk to Sulbha.*) Ah, Sulbha. Has Rani gone to school?

SULBHA: Yes.

MOHAN: Is Subhash busy with some case today?

SULBHA: Hmm. Yes.

MOHAN: You all right? Good. I am in a bit of a hurry today. (*He moves away to the left as Sulbha goes past the nursing home.*)

Sulbha approaches the back lawn from a side entrance. Maya is seen in the background, outside the kitchen complex, giving instructions to the servant as she walks towards the kitchen door.

MAYA: Ramu, go and get some almonds. I want to make a sweet dish for Rani.

RAMU: Yes, Bai.* (*He crosses Maya as he goes in the opposite direction.*)

Sulbha enters the back lawn and sits down on a stone seat, with her back to the camera. A postman comes with a registered letter.

POSTMAN: Registered letter, Bai. Here, sign here. (*She signs.*) Thank you. (*He leaves.*)

Sulbha starts reading the letter as she rises and walks away from the camera.

*A term of respect for women, used mainly by less educated and socially inferior people.

Sulbha comes towards the camera, reading the letter with great con-
centration. She sits on the large wooden swing in the foreground and
looks thoughtfully in front of her. The music swells, and the camera
closes in on her face. She sighs, deep in thought, then looks down at
the letter again.

The family at dinner in the dining room. Rani sits at one end of the
table, fussing over her food. On her left is Maya, who is coaxing her
to finish her meal. Sulbha sits on the right. Mohan appears from the
left, and walks up to the child, talking to her.

MOHAN: My sweet little one, you're not eating without me?
MAYA: She is not eating at all.
MOHAN: And why won't she eat? Come on darling, take something!
   It will drop! Uh huh!
MAYA: Now look how she is eating!

Mohan coaxes Rani to eat her meal. Sulbha watches unhappily from
the other side, then starts eating herself.

MOHAN: Now chew, chew, chew it well, my love. Aah! (*He opens his
   mouth wide to coax her to do the same.*)

Mohan and Rani face the camera. Maya is seen at Rani's left. Another
mouthful goes into Rani.

MAYA: Aah! (*She too opens her mouth wide as Rani obliges by accepting a
   mouthful grudgingly.*)
MOHAN: And this one for Aunty!

Sulbha watches the performance put up by Rani and her aunt and
uncle. She frowns.

Having achieved this much, Mohan moves towards his own chair,
leaving Maya to feed Rani.

MOHAN: Huh. Aunty, now you feed her.
MAYA: Ah, hah! (*as she feeds the child*).

Nani sits at the other end of the table. Subhash sits on the left. Mohan
enters the frame to sit on the right. As they talk among themselves, a
liveried servant serves the meal, takes instructions from Nani, and
moves away.

SUBHASH: Why are you so late, Mohan?

MOHAN: Nothing special. A delivery case. May have to do a Caesarean. Just preparing for that.

NANI: Come on, you have your meal. You may have to go back early.

MOHAN: Right.

SUBHASH: Yes, now you concentrate on him.

Rani is being difficult again.

MAYA: Why are you behaving like this, Rani dear?

SULBHA: Look, Rani, if you don't want to eat, you can leave. There must be a limit to your moods. (*Rani starts wailing at once.*)

MAYA: Let her stay. She'll remain hungry otherwise. (*Consoling Rani, who continues to wail.*) Oh no, no. Are you feeling sleepy? Very sleepy? Don't dear, don't! That's why I told you to eat earlier. No, no, there, there! (*Sulbha lowers her head once again, withdrawing herself.*)

Subhash and Nani at the other end of the table.

NANI (*sternly*): Make her stop that noise.

SUBHASH: Vahini,* if she doesn't want to eat, let her go.

Maya stands behind the child, pleading with her.

SULBHA: Rani!

MAYA: Very well, I'll take her away. Come on Rani, very sleepy, aren't you? Come along, you're sleepy. No, no, don't cry. (*She takes Rani with her, past Mohan, towards the door.*)

MOHAN: There, there, don't cry.

Subhash looks sternly at the camera, towards Sulbha.

MOHAN (*off*): My sweet baby!

MAYA (*off*): Shall I tell you a story?

Sulbha looks towards Subhash.

MOHAN (*off*): Go and sleep with Aunty.

Nani and Mohan at their end of the table.

*Sister-in-law.

NANI: That's the end of Maya's meal.

MOHAN: Let her go. If she is happy, why are you worrying about it? Let her go.

NANI: They are so attached to each other. She looks after the child more than her mother does. Who knows what she would have done had Rani been her own child!

Subhash turns towards Sulbha, who is out of the frame.

SUBHASH: You go to her and send Vahini back.

Mohan faces the camera.

MOHAN: Stop worrying. Maya likes it.

Subhash looks towards Sulbha.

SUBHASH: Why don't you go?

Subhash watches, as at the other end of the table Sulbha rises and moves away.

Sulbha enters Maya's room where Rani can be heard giggling. Camera moves with Sulbha to the bed where Rani lies, with Maya sitting beside her.

SULBHA: Rani, what's happening?

MAYA: She is listening to a story.

SULBHA: Let Aunty go and eat.

MAYA: Let it be!

SULBHA: Come now—

RANI: No.

A closer view of Sulbha as she sits on the bed beside Rani. Maya still sits on the left.

SULBHA: Rani, are you angry with me?

RANI (*putting her arms round her mother*): No.

SULBHA: My sweet Ranu! Maya, go and finish your dinner. Don't leave it half-way. Go on.

A close view of Maya facing the camera.

MAYA: I'll have it later. She has just quietened down.

A view of the bed with Maya sitting on the left. Sulbha stands by the bed, holding Rani.

SULBHA: Hmm. Come on, I'll tell you a story.

RANI (*turning and making a lunge for Maya, who holds her, looking pleased*): No, I don't like your stories. I like Aunty's story!

SULBHA: You are a spoilt child, aren't you? Hurry up now.

RANI (*still clinging to Maya*): No.

MAYA: Let her be. She can sleep here. Let her sleep here. I'll tell a story. A nice story. All right? What story shall I tell Rani today?

RANI: A nice one! Aha! (*Sulbha gives up and moves away to the right as Maya begins her story.*)

Sulbha walks into the drawing room. Through the door behind her, Maya can be seen telling Rani a story. As Sulbha walks into the room, the men can be heard talking to their mother. Sulbha walks towards the camera, then through a door into her own room.

MAYA: Once there was a king—

MOTHER (*off*): Politics is becoming senseless day by day.

MOHAN (*off*): How can you say that, Nani? There's a difference between politics and political leaders. Politics has remained the same. It is the leaders who have changed for the worse.

MOTHER (*off*): Subhash, have some curds.

SUBHASH (*off*): No, thanks. And, Nani, what about your own field of work? How many people are there in social work who are as sincere as you are?

MOHAN (*off*): And take the medical profession. That too is considered a sort of social work. But there too people are involved in so many rackets.

Camera moves as Sulbha walks towards the head of the bed, near the window, where she sits and lights the lamp.

Nani's end of the table. She talks to her sons as she eats. Subhash sits on the left as before, and Mohan on the right.

NANI: Subhash, I have always felt that my younger daughter-in-law should join me. She has a degree in social work, and we need a good, trained teacher for our adult education class. But she is not interested.

Subhash in close up, addresses his mother.

SUBHASH: Forget it, Nani. She doesn't want to do that sort of work. Haven't I told you before that she says that her subject for specialization was a different one?

Nani at her end of the table. She looks up sharply at Subhash.

NANI: What specialization did I have? And am I not running four or five institutions? (*She turns to Mohan as she speaks.*)

Maya and Rani in Maya's bedroom. Rani lies beside Maya, who reclines on the bed.

RANI: But what happens after that, Aunty?

Another view of Maya and the child on the bed. Maya faces the camera.

MAYA: Then the prince mounted his horse and went to hunt in the jungle.

Rani and Maya on the bed.

RANI: I don't want this story.
MAYA: Why?
RANI: It rains, and it gets dark, and the prince loses his way in the jungle. I don't want this story.
MAYA: No?
RANI: No. (*Maya laughs.*)

Maya and Rani from another angle. Maya thinks of another story.

MAYA: Hmm. Alibaba?
RANI: No, Aunty. There'll be forty thieves.
MAYA (*laughs*): No? Hmm. Then what story shall I tell you?
RANI: Which one, Aunty?
MAYA: Yes! Laurel and Hardy? Huh?
RANI: Yes! (*They both laugh happily.*)

A close view of Rani giggling with delight.

Subhash enters his bedroom, pulls the curtains together behind him, closes the door. He walks left to the desk near the bed where Sulbha still sits silently. Subhash looks at the papers on the desk as he starts speaking to her.

SUBHASH: After dinner, if you sit and talk to us for a while, it wouldn't do you any harm. Nani wants to talk to you. You think no end of yourself...

Subhash in the foreground, right of frame. Sulbha can be seen looking towards him, reclining against a pillow, with her knees drawn up. Subhash looks at her briefly as he talks, then turns back to the papers.

SUBHASH: ... ever since you completed the social work course. Earlier you had some communication with everybody at home.

Subhash stands near the table. Sulbha bows her head with a brief sigh as she listens to him.

SUBHASH: You've even moved away from Vahini. She is fond of you. You could complete a two-year course in Bombay only because of her. She has no child. She is unhappy.

Subhash walks from the foreground towards the bed as he talks. He reaches the other side of the bed, near another window, and sits on the bed with his papers.

SUBHASH: Mohan's profession keeps him fully occupied every hour of the day. We should try to understand Vahini. (*He puts on his glasses, then turns to look at Sulbha.*) Aren't you going to sleep?

SULBHA: Hmm. Not yet.

SUBHASH (*taking off his glasses absent-mindedly as he speaks*): If you would only assist Nani in her work, it would help you to get out of your present state of mind. But—but you are not doing anything at all, Sulu, you are just...

A close view of Sulbha looking up towards Subhash, who moves into the frame from the left, holds her close and lightly caresses her as he speaks.

SUBHASH: ... rotting, sitting here at home! Listen, shall we go out somewhere for a few days? Hmm? You'll feel better. I really mean it. I want to see you happy. Well?

SULBHA (*stiffly*): What should I say? Thank you? (*Subhash moves away, rebuffed.*)

SUBHASH: The household will carry on somehow. It does for everyone. A man may derive satisfaction from his wife's body. But, Sulu, that is not everything. (*He puts away his glasses and lies down on the bed as he speaks, looking away from Sulbha. She stares at the ceiling.*)

In Maya's room, Maya pulls the blanket over Rani, who is asleep, then slides under the blanket herself. She turns off the bedside lamp, and puts an arm round Rani before going to sleep.

Sulbha sits as before, awake, in the light of the lamp beside the bed, while Subhash sleeps, turned away from her. She looks at him, then gets up and goes to the desk, and takes out a letter from the drawer. She hesitates, then moves back to the bed and tries to wake Subhash. He turns towards her in his sleep. Sulbha looks at the letter again, then moves back to her pillow and turns off the lamp.

Morning. A close view of Subhash shaving, with a cigarette hanging from his lips. A Hindustani classical song is heard playing loudly on the radio. It is a mirror image. As the camera draws back, we see Subhash sitting in front of the dressing table mirror. Sulbha is seen in the mirror, at the back of the room, arranging clothes in the cupboard.

Sulbha takes a fresh bedcover from the cupboard, moves to the desk and pushes the chair under it, puts away a file, turns down the radio, lays the bedcover on the bed, and coming closer to the camera, picks up a sari to fold, looking hesitant.

View from behind Subhash. His face can be seen in the mirror. Sulbha comes up to him from the back, looking as if she would like to say something.

SUBHASH (*looking up at her through the mirror*): Hmm?

A close view of Sulbha looking disturbed.

Subhash looks at her through the mirror.

SUBHASH: What is it?
SULBHA: Nothing.
SUBHASH: Do you want to tell me something? You have been looking at me for a long time—
SULBHA: No.
SUBHASH: Hmm.

Subhash opens the bathroom door and peers out. He has just had a bath and has obviously yet to dry himself.

SUBHASH (*loudly*): Sulu! Towel—quick!

SULBHA (*off*): Coming!

Camera moves to Sulbha in another part of the room, laying out Subhash's clothes on the bed. She goes towards the bathroom carrying a towel.

SULBHA: What is this, Subhash? You are always . . .

SUBHASH (*grabbing her and trying to pull her into the bathroom*): Hey, come on!

SULBHA (*extricating herself*): What is this—— early in the morning——

SUBHASH: Just one minute. (*He pleads with her, but she moves away to the right.*)

SULBHA: Hurry up now!

Night. The lawn in front of the house. The family, seen from a distance, sitting around a table with fruits laid out. Nani sits to the left. On her left is Sulbha; next to her, Subhash. Mohan sits a little to the right, and Maya on his left, with her back to the camera. A table lamp stands on a small table between Sulbha and Subhash. Nani drinks from a glass. Subhash lights Mohan's cigarette and then his own as Mohan speaks.

MOHAN: Subhash!

SUBHASH: Hmm?

MOHAN: Your case is being talked about a lot these days.

SUBHASH: Which case?

MOHAN: The one with the doctor.

SUBHASH: Yes, yes.

MOHAN: Somebody was mentioning it in the hospital. What's it all about?

SUBHASH: You see, one of my clients, a doctor, is supposed to have raped a woman patient. That's the charge against him.

MOHAN: What? I can hardly believe it! A doctor raping a woman patient? Is there any medical evidence for it?

A closer shot of Mohan in the foreground right, then Subhash and Sulbha to the left. Sulbha frowns at her husband.

SUBHASH: Yes. There is evidence, and it is very clear.

A close view of Maya.

> MAYA: That means she has been raped. But then how will you defend him?

Another shot of the group from Maya's point of view. Subhash on the right. Sulbha on the left, looking at him.

> SUBHASH: Very simple. We shall show that the woman herself is of a questionable character. And that's not difficult to prove.

A close view of Nani.

> NANI: How would you do that?

A close view of Subhash with the lamp on his left.

> SUBHASH: Nani, the woman is poor. Her husband is a paralytic, and they have two children to feed. So I am . . .

A close view of Sulbha, who lowers her head unhappily as Subhash speaks.

> SUBHASH (*off*): . . . going to try a clever trick.
> MAYA (*off*): A clever trick?

A close view of Maya, who leans forward.

> Maya: How?

A view of the entire group from a distance.

> SUBHASH: I shall call attention to the age of the second child as compared with the length of time the husband has been a paralytic.

A close view of Nani facing the camera.

> NANI: What was that? I can't understand it.

A close view of Mohan facing the camera.

> MOHAN: Here, Nani, I'll tell you. He has to show that her husband was paralysed before she became pregnant for a second time. And that means . . .

A close view of Sulbha listening to the conversation with her head lowered and a frown on her forehead.

MOHAN (*off*): . . . that she is a woman of loose character. (*He turns towards Subhash, who is out of the frame.*) Isn't that right?

A close view of Nani, still puzzled.

NANI: But how does that help him to counter the rape charge?

The group viewed from behind Maya and Mohan. Nani seen on the left, Sulbha in front, and Subhash on the right.

SUBHASH (*smugly*): Because it proves that the woman is already immoral. Also, there is no evidence of resistance to the rape. And she may be making a noise about it because she is poor and needs money.

NANI (*impressed*): That's really clever of you! (*She turns to Maya with a smile.*) Isn't it? (*Sulbha, who looks up at Nani's comment, places on the table in the centre the plate of fruits she had on her lap, and quietly walks away into the darkness of the garden.*)

MAYA: Yes, it is!

MOHAN: Wonderful, brother, wonderful!

NANI (*noticing Sulbha moving away*): Now what's the matter with her?

SUBHASH (*slightly hesitant*): Maybe she's not feeling well. (*They all look at Sulbha's receding shape.*)

Sulbha, looking disturbed, walks into her room. The camera moves with her to the desk, where she takes out the letter from the drawer as music swells. The camera moves with her as she paces up and down, till she stops to face the camera. Music softens and quickens as she goes past the dressing table to the window on the left of the bed.

Subhash walks into the room and lifts his eyebrows disapprovingly as he sees Sulbha, who is out of the frame. He turns to shut the door.

A close view of Sulbha, who looks back at him from the window.

Subhash, with his back to the camera, goes to the table, picks up a file, and putting on his glasses as he talks, settles down on the bed.

SUBHASH: Nani was wondering why you left so suddenly.

SULBHA (*sitting on the bed at his side, and offering the letter*): Look at this.

SUBHASH: Hmm? What is it?

SULBHA: Why don't you read it? (*Camera draws slowly closer to them.*)

SUBHASH (*reading aloud*): Sangamwadi Mahilashram Superintendent's post. (*He is ready to hand the letter back to her without reading any further.*) I see, so that's what you have been thinking about all day?

SULBHA: Subhash, I want your opinion.

SUBHASH: What opinion can I have? Write and tell them that it's not possible.

SULBHA: Why? Why should I tell them it is not possible?

SUBHASH: Are you going to accept the job then? Have you gone mad?

SULBHA (*earnestly*): Subhash, I am not joking. I want to take up this job.

SUBHASH (*sighing in exasperation*): But—listen. You feel uncomfortable in this household because you have no work here that would satisfy you. (*He looks at her.*) But to leave home and go and live in a village like a ghost—that's no solution.

SULBHA: Why like a ghost? What are you talking about? Subhash, I am taking Rani with me. (*Subhash turns away from her with a sigh and puts his glasses back in their case.*)

A close view of Sulbha half turned away from the camera, and Subhash turning to look at her.

SUBHASH: Which means that for your own selfish purposes, you are going to take that child away from this home, and from Vahini? (*He puts his arm round her.*) Sulu, you want to leave me too for the sake of just a job?

A close view of Sulbha facing the camera, looking up at Subhash, who is turned away from the camera.

SULBHA: It's not easy for me either. But Sangamwadi is not so very far from here. It's a distance of only two or three hundred miles. (*Subhash removes his arm from her shoulder and listens to her.*) Subhash, it is only because of you that I could go to Bombay and complete this course after my marriage, standing first in my class. I had a glimpse of the wider world outside. Now how can I spend my life here like this? I feel stifled here. (*She puts her head on Subhash's shoulder.*)

Subhash faces the camera, holding Sulbha close to him, stroking her hair.

SUBHASH: Sulu, we shall find some work for you right here.

A close view of Sulbha looking up at Subhash, who is turned away from the camera.

SULBHA: I've tried that already. But there isn't any suitable work, there really isn't! Women have been neglected by society for a long, long time . . .

SUBHASH (*interrupting*): And that's why you want to neglect your home?

SULBHA: No, Subhash! Subhash, look! This is the only institute near our home. I got this job without having to be obliged to anybody. I might also start such an institution here later. Subhash, I am only going away from home for a short while, and that too with Rani. (*Subhash moves away from her.*)

A view of Subhash and Sulbha on the bed. Subhash takes out his glasses, puts them on and opens the file.

SUBHASH (*with deliberation*): Rani will stay here. She has to go to school.

SULBHA: But, Subhash, there may be a better school there.

SUBHASH: Not like this one.

SULBHA (*giving up and turning away to face the camera*): All right. I will go alone.

SUBHASH (*turns to her and speaks loudly*): You are not going either! (*Sulbha looks at him. Lowering his voice.*) I am sorry. I didn't mean it that way. (*Sulbha turns away and stares at the bed. He takes off his glasses again and puts them in the case.*) If you have set your heart on it, then there is nothing more to discuss. But this is a matter that doesn't affect just you and me. It affects the whole family. We will have to take everybody's opinion.

SULBHA (*looking at Subhash again*): But, Subhash, I must let them know within two days—(*Subhash gets up from the bed, moving to the right and out of the frame as the camera closes in on Sulbha.*)

A close view of Subhash looking stern.

A close view of Nani looking equally serious.

Outside the room Sulbha stands against the wall, listening apprehensively.

A close view of Maya's face.

A close view of Mohan, who sits looking uncomfortable.

A view of the entire room showing Mohan sitting against a wall at the far end, with Maya standing next to him at the door of their room. Nani sits on the left. Sulbha can be seen hiding behind the door of her room, leaning against the wall, listening.

> NANI: Who am I to take a decision? It is up to you both to decide on the matter. I can't understand why she has to leave home to do social work when there is enough work to be done right here. And that too leaving you and your daughter behind.

A close view of Subhash, who replies cautiously.

> SUBHASH: No, she was quite prepared to take Rani with her. It is I who said 'no'.

A close view of Sulbha listening to the conversation in the next room.

> NANI (*off*): And how do you feel . . .

Nani seen from a distance, sitting turned away from the camera. The door to the porch can be seen in the background. Subhash stands facing Nani nearer the outer door. He moves towards Nani, who turns to look at him.

> NANI: . . . about her leaving?
> SUBHASH: Nani, we must try to understand her point of view. I think your kind of work would not satisfy her. She received a degree in social work from Bombay; came first in her class. So she can no longer sit idle at home like other women. She has got this job fairly easily, and it is the kind of work she is interested in. She feels this is an opportunity for her to demonstrate her capabilities.

Another view of the drawing room. Subhash on the left, Nani looking up at him. Mohan at the back, and Sulbha in her room, frowning as she listens.

NANI: And you agree?

SUBHASH: If I look at it from her viewpoint, yes.

NANI: Do women of respectable families leave their husband and home for the sake of a job?

Another view of Nani in the foreground, right, turning back to look at Subhash, who stands near her.

SUBHASH: But she is not leaving her home, Nani. She says that it is only a question of adjustment for a short period of time.

NANI: Don't give me a lawyer's arguments.

A close view of Sulbha, her eyes full of tears.

NANI (off): Do you accept it?

A close view of Subhash looking in Nani's direction. He speaks carefully.

SUBHASH: I accept it.

The drawing room from inside Sulbha's room.

NANI: That's fine then! (*Subhash walks towards the door in the foreground where Sulbha stands. He goes past the door to the right and stands with his back to the camera.*) As for me, I'll have my reply if people ask for an explanation. But it is you who will have to live like an ascetic even though you have a wife. And at such an early age. But I cannot understand . . .

A close view of Subhash, who frowns at Nani.

NANI (off): . . . how you can approve of such a decision!

A close view of Nani, who turns to Mohan.

NANI: What do you say, Mohan?

A close view of Subhash, who also turns towards Mohan.

MOHAN (off): Hmm?

Mohan is a little startled by Nani's question and shifts uncomfortably in his chair. As he relaxes again and starts speaking, Maya moves closer and stands by him, looking first at him, then at Nani, who is out of the frame.

> MOHAN: Well, Nani, if she wants to go, why don't you let her? What difference does it make? But it's for Subhash to decide really, isn't it?

A close view of Nani.

> NANI: If your Maya wanted to leave . . .

Mohan and Maya face the camera.

> NANI (*off*): . . . would you allow her to go away?
> MOHAN (*with an apologetic smile*): I really can't tell. Maybe I wouldn't let her go. It is difficult to accept such a situation, isn't it?

Nani in the foreground looks up at Subhash, who is out of the frame. Maya and Mohan can be seen at the back. She rises and walks towards Subhash as she speaks. The camera moves with her till she reaches him.

> NANI: Subhash, all I can say is, think it over before taking a final decision. I am old now. I have fulfilled all my duties to my home, been a daughter-in-law, a wife, and a mother. I have had a lot of problems. People cast doubts on my character and tried to poison my father-in-law's mind. I too had to go outside the home to work. But, Subhash . . .

A close view of Sulbha listening intently.

> NANI (*off*): . . . I did not leave my home!

Nani and Subhash standing together as before.

> SUBHASH: Yes, Nani. I won't come to any decision without thinking it over. (*Nani walks away through the door next to Subhash.*)

A close view of Subhash, who watches his mother leave, then moves to the right and out of the frame.

Sulbha comes into the bedroom from the dressing room, undoing her hair. She finds Subhash covering the sleeping Rani with a sheet.

SULBHA: Subhash! Let me do it! (*She hurries to the right of the bed.*)

SUBHASH: No, no, let it be. I must learn to do all this work now. (*Camera closes in on the bed to show Subhash looking after his daughter, then draws back to Sulbha again, who has dropped on her knees beside the bed and is sobbing into Subhash's lap.*) Oh! What's this? Huh? Come, get up. (*He pulls her up gently.*) You shouldn't cry like this! Why——

SULBHA: Subhash, thank you!

SUBHASH: Thank you? Hey, listen! Whatever I told Nani was not what I believe. I was only pleading your case.

SULBHA: I am lucky to have such a well-known lawyer fighting my case!

SUBHASH: But you'll pay for it, won't you?

SULBHA: Shall I? (*She sits on the bed now with her back to the camera, with Subhash holding her close as music swells and the camera draws closer.*)

Night. Sulbha and Rani lie sleeping on the bed. Subhash is reclining against the wall near the lamp, smoking thoughtfully in the dark. He lights the lamp and calls Sulbha.

SUBHASH: Sulu! Sulu!

SULBHA (*waking up*): What's the matter?

SUBHASH: Listen to me. I can well imagine how you feel. And I can understand it. I cannot shut my eyes to your unhappiness just because it suits my selfish interests. You can go. Without you, I will be unhappy. But that's all right——

SULBHA (*extending an arm to touch Subhash*): Subhash!

SUBHASH: But I have one condition. You should never say I have not given you the opportunity you wanted. (*Sulbha touches Rani to reassure her as she moves in her sleep.*) I know people will laugh and call me a fool for giving in to your wishes. Let them. That's all right by me. I'd rather be a fool than be cruel to you. Now go to sleep. (*He stubs out the cigarette, turns off the lamp and lies down with his back to her. Sitting up in the dark, she sighs.*)

Morning. Sulbha and Rani are sitting on the large wooden swing in the garden. Sulbha is combing Rani's hair while Rani reads aloud from a book. The shot opens with a close view of Rani alone.

RANI: This is me. I have a friend.

This is my mummy. She is my friend. (*Camera draws back to show Sulbha kissing Rani, who continues reading.*)
This is my daddy. He is my friend.

From the background, Maya approaches facing the camera. She stops to speak to them, then moves away.

MAYA: Sulbha, are you plaiting her hair?
SULBHA: Yes.
MAYA: All right. Rani, when you finish, come and have your milk.
RANI: Yes, I'll do that, Aunty.
SULBHA: Rani, I have to go away for a few days.
RANI: Why?
SULBHA: I have some work.
RANI: Then do your work here!
SULBHA: It cannot be done here. I'll have to go away for it.
RANI: Then will you come back tomorrow?

A view from a different angle. Rani faces the camera with Sulbha behind her, bending over her as she talks and ties a ribbon to Rani's hair.

SULBHA: I will have to stay away for many days.
RANI: Then all of us can go with you! You, me, Daddy, Aunty——

Another view of Sulbha and Rani, both seen in profile.

SULBHA: No, Rani, I have to go alone. Listen to me. (*Camera starts moving closer as Rani turns to look at her mother, who holds Rani's face between her hands as she speaks.*) Don't be any trouble to Aunty. And don't do anything to upset your father.
RANI (*tearfully*): But don't go! I am telling you——

Sulbha holds Rani's face away from her to look at her as she speaks.

SULBHA (*breaking down*): Listen to me—— Go to school every day. Drink your milk on time. And sleep with Aunty or your father. (*She pulls the child to her again as camera draws closer.*)

In their bedroom, Subhash dresses for work, adjusting the collar to put on his tie. The radio loudly plays a Hindustani classical song.

A close view of Sulbha arranging the bed. She looks towards Subhash, who is out of the frame.

He turns towards her, now out of the frame, as he puts on his tie, and turns down the collar.

A close view of Sulbha near the bed. She looks downwards.

A view of the room, with Subhash in front of the dressing table. He looks back at the bed where Sulbha, in foreground left, is laying out his coat. Sulbha opens a wooden box on the bed. Subhash suddenly, grimly, snatches away the coat.

SULBHA: What . . .?

SUBHASH (*bending to pick up his hairbrush*): My coat. (*She comes forward to help him put it on. He speaks brusquely.*) No, let it be. (*He starts brushing his hair.*)

SULBHA (*apologetically*): I was just going to give it to you.

She goes left, the camera following her, to the cupboard, from the top of which she tries to bring down a suitcase. It is a little too high and she turns to call Subhash, who is now out of the frame.

SULBHA: Subhash! Will you reach down my suitcase?

Subhash enters the frame from the right, places his bag and coat on the floor between the cupboard and the drawing room door, and lifts the suitcase, placing it in front of Sulbha. Sulbha tries to brush the dust off his shirt.

SUBHASH (*turning away quickly*): It's all right.

SULBHA (*stopping him with her hand on his arm*): But your shirt is dirty! Won't you change it?

SUBHASH (*turning back to Sulbha with a frown*): Let it be. (*He picks up his coat and bag.*)

SULBHA: Subhash! (*She holds his arm shyly. Maya appears at the door.*)

MAYA (*smiling*): Sulbha, will you give me Rani's clothes, toys and books now, so that there is no confusion afterwards?

SULBHA: Oh, yes.

SUBHASH: I'll get back early today. I'll come home directly from the court. You will be ready of course.

SULBHA: Subhash! (*He leaves without turning back.*)

Sulbha and Maya smile at each other, then Sulbha pulls Maya into the room.

MAYA: Finished all your preparations?

SULBHA (*bringing her to the cupboard*): They're going on. Oh yes. She

can't sleep without Subhash. If she starts crying . . . Oh here's
the nightie. (*She starts handing Maya clothes and toys as she speaks.*)
And her other things are in the cupboard. (*Disjointedly*) And she
wants french toast in the morning. Oh yes, here's a dress. Oh,
and *Birbal, Shyam's Mother* and *Aesop's Fables*, all three books are
torn. Will you get her new ones? Yes, I got this dress for her only
yesterday. It's for her birthday.

MAYA (*smiling at her with affection and compassion*): I know everything
now. Leave your worries behind when you go. All right? (*Maya
touches Sulbha's cheek. Moved by her concern, Sulbha smiles at her
gratefully.*)

In Nani's room, Nani dictates a letter to Deshpande. Deshpande sits
in the foreground, right, with his back to the camera. Nani looks at a
newspaper as she speaks.

NANI: Make it quite clear to them that we will help them in every
way, but they must raise the money for the building fund.

Sulbha enters from a door at the back, beyond the divan on which
Nani sits. She waits silently till Deshpande draws Nani's attention
to her.

DESHPANDE: Sulbhatai has come.

NANI (*looks at Sulbha, then back to the newspaper again*): Huh? What
is it?

SULBHA: Er, Nani, I am going this evening.

NANI: All right. Take care of your health. Write often.

SULBHA: Yes.

NANI (*to Deshpande*): Then, about the money—— (*Turns back to
dismiss Sulbha.*) All right, you can go. (*To Deshpande again*) Tell
them clearly—— will you read what I have said so far?

DESHPANDE: We can help you in all other ways, but the fund for
constructing a building will have to be raised by you. (*Sulbha
waits for a little while, then leaves.*)

NANI: Right.

DESHPANDE: All right?

NANI: Yes.

DESHPANDE: Next?

Subhash enters his room, drawing the curtains aside. Camera follows
him as he walks up to Sulbha, who is sobbing with her back to the

camera. As Subhash speaks, she wipes her eyes and turns.

SUBHASH: Are you ready? Let us go.

SULBHA: Yes.

SUBHASH: I think the luggage is outside already.

A close view of Subhash and Sulbha. They are both at a loss and unhappy. She turns towards him.

SULBHA: Yes.

A close view of Subhash looking uncomfortable.

A big close up of Sulbha in tears.

SULBHA: Where's Rani?

A close view of Subhash as before.

SUBHASH: I'll go and see.

Sulbha in a big close up.

SULBHA: No, let it be. She must be outside. Let us go.

A big close up of Subhash.

SUBHASH: All right.

Camera draws back to show Sulbha in tears, bending to touch her husband's feet.

SUBHASH (*pulling her up*): Hey! Hey Sulu! What are you doing? Get up, do! (*Camera comes closer as he holds her against him, consoling her as she weeps.*) You mustn't cry now, silly girl.

SULBHA: Will you take care of yourself?

SUBHASH: And you too. (*He tries to kiss her.*)

SULBHA (*turning her face away*): Un hunh, someone might see us.

SUBHASH: All right. Hurry back.

SULBHA: Yes, I will.

SUBHASH: Come, let us go——(*They move to the right and out of the frame.*)

View from the drawing room. Subhash draws apart the curtains of the door of his room as he and Sulbha enter the drawing room. He moves left and out of the frame while Sulbha goes to the middle of the room where Maya stands, holding a plate. Observing the formality of leavetaking, she touches Sulbha's forehead with something in her hand. Sulbha picks up a sweet from the plate, and puts it in her mouth before bending down to touch Maya's feet.

MAYA: No, no, no, why are you touching my feet? You should leave with a peaceful mind. Don't worry about anyone here. And I'll take care of Rani. She is playing somewhere outside. (*She puts the plate on a table and escorts Sulbha towards the outer door.*)

SULBHA: Outside?

MAYA: Come——

Rani can be seen at a distance, on the swing in the garden.

SULBHA (*off*): Rani!

Camera draws back as she jumps off the swing and hops across the hedges, running towards the voice.

RANI: Mummy! Mummy!

SULBHA (*off*): Rani!

The car stands near the porch. Rani rushes in from the left. Sulbha sweeps her up in her arms, watched by Subhash. Sulbha is sobbing.

RANI: Mummy, why are you crying? Listen to me——

SULBHA: Rani! (*Camera moves closer to Rani and Sulbha.*)

A close view of Subhash watching grimly.

A close view of Sulbha and Rani, both weeping.

A close view of Maya approaching Sulbha. Camera draws back to show Maya taking Rani from Sulbha. Subhash gets into the driver's seat and shuts the door. Sulbha goes past the bonnet towards the other door, then runs back to kiss Rani where she stands with Maya by the car.

SULBHA: Rani, don't give Aunty any trouble, all right? I'll come back soon. Ta ta! (*She moves once more towards the other door of the car.*)

A close view of Subhash through the car window, looking out towards Rani, who is out of the frame, as he starts the car.

3

A close view of Rani's tearful face.

Another close view of Subhash.

Rani's face as she looks on tearfully.

View from a distance of the car driving off as Maya and Rani stand waving.

View of Maya and Rani from the moving car receding in the distance. The gates of the house are left behind as the car moves forward.

A train approaches from far right and moves left past the camera, by a railway platform.

The guard strikes a sheet of metal that passes for a bell, announcing the arrival of the train.

Sulbha comes out of her compartment with her suitcase. She looks around, then looks at her watch. There is obviously no one to fetch her. She picks up the suitcase and walks away to the right.

Sulbha, seen from a distance, coming out of the small nondescript station. She comes down the steps as a villager goes up past her. The camera pans as she moves towards a *tonga* standing outside. She talks to the driver.

SULBHA: I want to go to the Mahilashram.

DRIVER (*taking the suitcase from her*): Come and sit in the *tonga*.

He puts the suitcase in the cart, and mounts the driver's seat. Sulbha sits on the passenger seat at the back, which faces in the opposite direction. The *tonga* driver shakes his stick at the horse, and the journey begins.

A series of shots showing the path taken by the *tonga*. Green bushes and jungles, a little culvert leading to a dirt track through a barren landscape. Close ups of the *tonga* with Sulbha facing the camera, the horse and the driver, the horse's hooves moving in steady rhythm. A train approaches the camera down a railway track, along which runs a road. The camera draws closer to the *tonga* on the road as the train

rushes past. The *tonga* jolts along a road lined with tall trees. Sulbha
sits looking serious and apprehensive. The sun suddenly appears from
behind the curtain of leaves and branches. Now the *tonga* moves into
the narrow winding lanes of the little town, past low brick shanties, to
a road past a long wall, with sloping tiled roofs beyond. The wall ends
in a porch where the *tonga* stops at last. It is the Mahilashram.
Throughout, on the sound-track, a song is heard.

> *Song (off)*: Let my rusted lips
> > feel the sharpness of God's thunder,
> Let my blind soul
> > be burned by the sun of truth.
> Let the dry bones of my body
> > be permeated by the happiness that beauty brings,
> Let my very being
> > spread a fragrance while it burns.
> Let the old ones
> > live humbly in the shade,
> But let my sweat fall upon the burning ground
> > with dignity.

The song ends as the *tonga* stops in front of the porch of the Mahilashram. The signboard reads 'Sheth Dindayal Jagatram's Home for
Destitute Women, Sangamwadi, Dt. Dharampur'. Sulbha gets off
the *tonga* and puts her suitcase on the ground.

SULBHA: How much?
DRIVER: Four rupees.
SULBHA: Here. (*She pays him.*)
DRIVER: *Ram Ram.** (*To the horse*) Hey! Come on! (*He moves away
with the cart.*)

Sulbha walks up to the large wooden gates of the Mahilashram. The
gates are firmly shut. Sulbha bends and pushes the wicket gate.

View from inside the Mahilashram. A small table with some registers
and a chair beside it in front of the wicket gate, to the left of the
frame. The wicket gate opens as Sulbha bends to enter. There is a
second inner gate which is wide open. Sulbha comes in with her
shoulder bag, then brings the suitcase in and walks towards the

---

*A common greeting, taking the name of the legendary Lord Rama, and
signifying, 'God be with you.'

camera, looking around. Camera moves with her to the edge of the inner gate, to the right. A notice board and a door to a room can be seen in the space between the two gates. Sulbha stops as she hears a shout. The gatekeeper and Kamlabai come running up to Sulbha.

GATEKEEPER: Hey! Stop right there! Who do you want? What brings you here?

KAMLABAI (*To the gatekeeper*): Hey! She looks young.

GATEKEEPER: Oh they are always young. You can't go beyond this point till you fill in the register. (*He goes towards the table, out of the frame, as he speaks, returning with the register.*) First fill in the register. Here. Hmm. (*He hands the register and a pen to Sulbha and reads her entry as she hands it back to him with a frown. Suddenly he is all attention.*) Salaam, Baisaheb!* Hey Kamlabai! What are you waiting for? It's our new Superintendent Baisaheb! Let the attendants know! Go on! (*Duly impressed, Kamlabai rushes away.*)

SULBHA (*sternly*): Didn't you know that I was coming?

GATEKEEPER: Oh, Baisaheb, er, um, that peon, he went . . . Come on, come on. (*He picks up her suitcase and goes ahead of her. Camera moves to follow them into the courtyard of the Mahilashram.*) Hey! Hurry up, Kamlabai, hurry up!

A wide open courtyard, with part of a well and washing space visible on the left where three girls can be seen. Girls in pink, pale green and yellow saris and an attendant in white are seen variously engaged. The buildings loom menacingly at the back, ugly and standardized grey brick barracks, with sloping tiled roofs and awnings, and a bright streak of white paint below the windows. Camera pans to show the well in the centre, and to the right more barracks, some trees, and many more girls.

Kamlabai brings Sulbha to her quarters. They enter a small passage, to the right of which is the bedroom. View from the bedroom. Kamlabai and Sulbha stop at the bedroom door. The suitcase is on the floor on the right of the door, and a chair stands further right. A steel cupboard stands on the left, beside the window, and near a table. In the foreground, mattresses can be seen folded on a utilitarian bed with a metal frame and strips of canvas stretched across it.

Salaam, originally an Arabic word meaning 'Peace', is used as a greeting, often accompanied by a salute. *Saheb* is the equivalent of 'sir', denoting additional respect.

KAMLABAI: Come in, Bai. The former Bai used to occupy this room. The bathroom is outside. Shall I get you some breakfast?

SULBHA (*surveying the room*): Hmm? Oh no.

KAMLABAI (*smiling*): Would you like some tea?

SULBHA (*turns to her*): Are you in charge of the kitchen here?

KAMLABAI (*stops smiling*): No, Bai. I am the head inmate here.

SULBHA: So that means you are one of the women who live in this place. Please send the person in charge of the kitchen to me.

KAMLABAI: All right.

One of the girls peering in through the outer door disengages herself from the crowd and comes towards the inner room with folded hands and a smile.

SATYABHAMABAI: I am Satyabhamabai. I am in charge of the kitchen here. Can I get you something?

SULBHA: No, I don't want anything. You can go back to your work.

Kamlabai and Satyabhamabai leave, taking the curious crowd with them. Sulbha sits down on the chair and looks around the room.

Gulab and Bakula, two of the inmates, come across the courtyard towards the camera and join a queue where girls stand fidgeting, whispering, battling silently with each other. The camera pans to show two attendants—Satyabhamabai seated under a tree, and Rukminibai standing by her—distributing washing soap and hair oil to the girls. A very young girl in an advanced state of pregnancy, Mangala, walks down the queue towards the camera after receiving her quota.

A GIRL: Hey! Come on, hurry up! Hurry up!

RUKMINIBAI: Come on, take it, quickly.

SATYABHAMABAI: Name, tell me your name!

RUKMINIBAI: Tell her!

SATYABHAMABAI: Come on—your name?

View from behind the attendants as the distribution continues.

RUKMINIBAI: Hey, run along now. (*To another girl*) Use the soap sparingly. Every two days you want a new cake of soap, eh? You procuress!

A portion of the queue where two girls get into a violent quarrel and try to literally tear each other's hair.

RUKMINIBAI (*off*): Come, hold it!

JASWANDI: What? Wait a minute, you bitch! You are becoming too clever, aren't you?

GIRL: You are a bitch! (*They go for each other's hair, abusing each other shrilly, the words indistinguishable in the general cacophony.*)

Sulbha in the distance, walking across the space between two buildings. She stops at the noise of the quarrel.

Sulbha's view of the fighting girls. A girl walks towards the camera with her rations while the battle rages in the distance.

Jangam, Sunanda, and a third girl in view. Jangam's face falls as she notices Sulbha, who is out of the frame.

Sulbha stands looking in the direction of the quarrel.

Keeping her eyes on Sulbha, who is out of the frame, Jangam moves towards the quarrelling girls.

ONE OF THE GIRLS: . . . you're showing off all the time!

JANGAM: Hey! Bai has come! Bai! Bai!

The girls promptly separate and look innocently towards where Sulbha stands out of the frame.

A closer view of Sulbha, who still stands where she was, watching the girls.

Jangam moves away and Jaswandi and the other girl start moving with the queue again.

Sulbha stands looking in their direction.

Satyabhamabai and Rukminibai under the tree, doling out the rations.

SATYABHAMABAI: Come on, keep to the line!

RUKMINIBAI (*who has spotted Sulbha in the distance*): Bai is coming.

Satyabhamabai takes a quick look in Sulbha's direction.

Her view of Sulbha, who stands as before.

Satyabhamabai stands up and continues her count of the girls and the rations given to them. She is more subdued, and glances uncomfortably towards Sulbha.

Sulbha stands watching, then turns away and moves towards the left.

Another view of the courtyard. On the right girls are washing huge cooking vessels near the well. On the left a girl sits playing with her child under a tree. Other girls can be seen in the background, sitting or moving against the barrack walls. Sulbha is seen walking into this area from between two barracks. She comes towards the well. Some girls who were sitting and talking quickly jump down from their perch when Sulbha passes them. The girls washing vessels stand up to greet her.

ONE GIRL: Bai is here.
ALL THE GIRLS: *Namaste.*

Sulbha returns the greeting and walks past them to the left.

Sulbha's office viewed from inside. Through a window on the right Sulbha is seen walking towards the door. Between the window and the door the peon sits yawning and crushing tobacco in his palm. Girls gather around to watch as Sulbha enters the office. The peon springs to attention.

Sulbha sits at her desk; there is a table lamp on the left and a telephone on the right. A triangular piece of wood set in the middle announces that the person who sits there is the Superintendent. There is the usual assortment of objects on the table, like rubber stamps, a penholder, a pincushion, and a large blotting pad. Sulbha looks up towards the peon.

SULBHA: Hmm. You are the peon, aren't you?

The peon salutes her smartly.

PEON: Yes Bai. I am Doiphode.

A closer view of Sulbha.

SULBHA: Tell the girls standing outside to go to their own barracks.

The peon nods and turns to the door to shout at the girls gathered outside.

PEON: Yes. Hey girls! Don't hang around here! It's Baisaheb's orders. Go to your barracks. Off you go! (*He comes back towards Sulbha, smiling in triumph.*) They've gone, Baisaheb.

A closer view of Sulbha looking stern.

SULBHA: Weren't you supposed to go to the railway station this morning to receive me?

The peon moves towards the desk as he speaks. Sunanda, one of the inmates, can be seen sitting at a typewriter in one corner of the room.

PEON (*with growing discomfort*): Er, yes, er, no Baisaheb. Actually we just missed each other. But I searched for you up and down, Baisaheb!

View over the peon's shoulder. Sulbha sits looking sternly at him.

SULBHA: Were you there when the train arrived at the platform?

View over Sulbha's shoulder. The peon looks embarrassed. Sunanda in the background.

PEON: Yes, yes, Baisaheb. But I was just a little late, Baisaheb. (*He is smiling ingratiatingly.*)

View over the peon's shoulder.

SULBHA: You were not there at the station.

The peon tries once again to convince Sulbha. View over Sulbha's shoulder.

PEON: I was there, Baisaheb. (*He pinches the skin near his Adam's apple.*) I swear by God!
SULBHA: You can go. (*He salutes and turns away.*)

The peon moves away to the right. Sulbha sits facing the camera, looking stern. Then her face softens as she turns to the girl at the typewriter, who is out of the frame.

SULBHA: What is your name?

A closer view of Sunanda.

SUNANDA: Sunanda Hirwe.

A similar view of Sulbha.

SULBHA: Hmm. Look, do something for me. Prepare a notice: the girls of the Ashram should not neglect their work and hang around the office. And the gatekeeper must not go anywhere leaving his post.

SUNANDA: All right.

View from inside Sulbha's office. The gatekeeper runs in at the door.

GATEKEEPER: Chairmanbai has come. (*He runs out again.*)

A closer view of Sulbha, who rises.

A jeep stands in front of the open veranda skirting the rooms in one section of the courtyard. Mrs Samson, the chairperson of the Managing Committee of the Ashram, stands before the jeep, facing right. Sulbha walks into the frame from the right, and greets her. They climb the steps of the veranda where a table and a chair are kept. A steel water jar stands on the table with a steel glass covering its mouth. Mrs Samson sits at the table. Sulbha stands facing her. A large gong hangs from the sloping roof of the veranda just behind Sulbha.

SULBHA: *Namaste.*

MRS SAMSON: *Namaste.* Did you arrive this morning?

SULBHA: Yes.

MRS SAMSON: That's good. We have all been waiting for you. You've come alone, haven't you?

A close view of Sulbha.

SULBHA: Yes. I've come alone.

Another view of Sulbha and Mrs Samson. Sulbha stands in the foreground on the right, partially turned away from the camera. Mrs Samson sits on the left.

MRS SAMSON: I have to attend a meeting right now. But before doing that I thought I should give you some idea about how this place is run. (*Turning to the driver, who is out of the frame.*) Driver! Bring my thermos here. I want some water.

A close view of Sulbha near the gong. She turns towards the car and back again.

Sulbha and Mrs Samson seen together. Sulbha stands turned away from the camera.

MRS SAMSON (*talking briskly*): Every day you should give me a report of your activities over the telephone. As I am the chairperson, you will have to take my permission for everything. (*The driver pours out water from the flask. Mrs Samson drinks.*) The Managing Committee meets every three months. You should consult me before setting a date for it. I have to check the date with the District Superintendent of Police and the Collector before arranging for the meeting. (*She rises and walks past Sulbha to the steps as she speaks.*) Ring me after nine at night. Or if it's urgent, in the evening at the Officers' Club. But I generally don't like being disturbed. (*She goes to the jeep followed by Sulbha, then turns back again.*) Oh yes, there have been many complaints from the staff about that girl, Utpala Joshi. Keep her case history ready for the next meeting.

She gets into the jeep, which reverses as the camera moves behind Sulbha, who stands watching. The camera pans to show the jeep going forward and away, when voices are heard in the background. Sulbha turns and walks towards the noise.

KAMLABAI (*off, screaming*): You abandoned creature! What's going on here? Is this your father's property?

MUKTA (*off*): Shut up, Kamlabai.

Close up of Mukta looking grim. Camera draws back to reveal Kamlabai surrounded by a group of girls in the larder.

KAMLABAI (*facing Mukta*): Hey you little blowpipe, with whose permission have you been touching anything here? (*She tries to shake Mukta.*)

MUKTA (*shaking off Kamlabai's hand*): Hey! Don't touch me, you whore!

KAMLABAI: You are a whore.

SHOBHA: We know all about what your husband and daughter are up to.

KAMLABAI (*turning to Shobha and speaking with sarcasm*): Oh? And who have you been sleeping with, you bitch?

ANOTHER GIRL: Let's give her a thrashing. She talks too much.
KAMLABAI (*turning to her*): You shut up!

Sulbha appears between two stacks of firewood where two girls stand watching the battle in the kitchen. They run away as the camera pans with Sulbha, who walks into the room.

SULBHA: What's going on here?
KAMLABAI: She is being rude to me.
SULBHA: What kind of behaviour is this, huh? Who is in charge of the kitchen?
KAMLABAI (*sulkily*): Satyabhamabai.
SULBHA: Then what are you doing with the keys?
KAMLABAI: The keys have been with me from before Satyabhamabai's time.
SULBHA: Give me the keys. (*Kamlabai does not respond.*) Hand those keys to me! (*Kamlabai reluctantly parts with the keys of the kitchen while the girls stand watching.*) From now on the keys will remain with Satyabhamabai. Do you understand? You can go. (*Kamlabai walks off in a huff.*)

Three girls face the camera.

SULBHA (*off*): Your names?
MUKTA: Mukta Gaekwad.
UTPALA: Utpala Joshi.
SHOBHA: Shobha Lokhande.

Another view of the group, this time including Sulbha on the right.

SULBHA: Hmm. What are you doing here?
MUKTA: Today it is our turn to cook. We came to take the rice and the wheat.
SULBHA: Then?
UTPALA: That Kamlabai always shouts at us. She tells me that I am pregnant without being married. I know what kind of a saint she is—clean as a washed grain of rice!
KAMLABAI (*off*): You shrew!

Close up of Kamlabai gesticulating near the woodpile.

KAMLABAI: Don't you say anything behind my back!

Sulbha with the girls. She turns towards Kamlabai, who is out of the frame.

SULBHA: Kamlabai, didn't I tell you to leave?

Kamlabai near the woodpile. She walks off in a huff.

KAMLABAI (*with disdain*): Hah!

Sulbha stands near the three girls.

SHOBHA (*to Kamlabai, who is out of the frame*): Whatever you want to say, go and say it to your whore of a daughter!

SULBHA: Stop it!

UTPALA: The previous Superintendent allowed her a lot of freedom. Why not? She was a great help to her—supplying girls to Madan Seth.

MUKTA (*nudging Utpala*): Hush.

SULBHA: All right. Now go to your own rooms. Go on. (*The girls disperse. Camera closes in on Sulbha.*)

The door of the tailoring class. Sulbha walks in. Camera moves with her to the teacher at the desk.

TEACHER: *Namaste.*

SULBHA: *Namaste.* (*She turns towards the class.*)

Sulbha's view of the class. The girls rise from their sewing machines to greet her together.

GIRLS (*all together*): *Namaste.*

Sulbha and the teacher. Sulbha walks towards the camera down rows of girls working at their sewing machines. She stops in front of a girl who sits staring idly in front of her.

SULBHA (*as she walks*): Sit down, sit down. There is no need to stand up whenever I come here. You go on with your work. (*Stopping in front of the girl who sits idle*) What's your name?

A GIRL: She is deaf and dumb, Bai.

TEACHER (*off*): Her name is Kusum Shinde, Bai.

A close view of Sulbha's face to the right of the frame, looking at

Kusum as the teacher recounts her story. Both Kusum and the teacher are out of the frame.

> TEACHER (*off*): She has been like that since her birth. Once when there was nobody at home, three boys . . .

Close up of Kusum, who looks up, then lowers her head again.

> TEACHER (*off*): . . . of the area came and raped her. Since then . . .

A close view of the teacher.

> TEACHER: . . . she behaves like this.

Kusum, her head lowered.

> TEACHER (*off*): If she feels like it, she works, otherwise she sits like this.

Sulbha's profile to the right of the frame. She lowers her head silently, then moves away.

As Sulbha comes out of the tailoring class, a mad girl lunges at her, catching hold of her arm.

> MAD GIRL: Did you see the snake? Black! Black! Poisonous! It climbs all over my body. Oh, oh! It has come. Take it away! Kill it!

Sulbha struggles to loosen the mad girl's grip as they move past an empty room to an open courtyard where others gather. Satyabhamabai, Mangala and another girl are in the foreground left. Rukminibai comes from the right and takes the mad girl away.

> RUKMINIBAI: She is mad, Bai. She lost her mind after her marriage. Her husband was like a demon. She was terrified of him. (*She takes the girl away.*)
> A GIRL (*with an insinuating smile*): Go on! What was there to be terrified of? It's just that some men are a bit rough. (*She moves away.*)

Camera moves closer to Sulbha, who turns to look at the girl, still recovering from the shock of the mad girl's assault. She moves away to the right.

Sulbha walks past the high outer walls of the Mahilashram. She wipes her face with the end of her sari, looking thoughtful. She stops where a tree casts its shadow on the the wall, looks up at the wall's immense height, then moves on to the right as the camera pans with her.

A close view of Sulbha inside her living quarters. It is night. She wipes the dust off a framed picture of Subhash, and puts it back beside another picture frame which holds three small photographs of Rani. Camera pans with her as she pulls back her hair, rubs her face with her hands, and moves to the right. She sits down on the bed, pushing up the pillow against the headboard, and cleans her glasses. On a small table beside the bed, a lighted table lamp. Sulbha puts on her glasses, and leaning against the pillow, picks up a thick pile of folders and turns a page.

A close view of the folder, showing a photograph of Kamlabai, and another, presumably, of her family. The camera shows, over Sulbha's shoulder, her hand holding a pen, turning the page.

A close view of Sulbha as she reads. She turns towards the camera as the gatekeeper's call is heard.

The gatekeeper, who doubles for a watchman at night, is out on his rounds. A view from the top. In the distance, in the dimly lit courtyard, he can be seen moving around near the well.

GATEKEEPER (*shouting*): A—ll right! Everything is a—ll right!

Inside her room, Sulbha turns back to her reading.

A lamp glowing near the high wall on the left. The barracks on the right. The gatekeeper appears again, striking the ground with his stick and repeating his cry.

Camera faces Sulbha in a close up. She turns a page.

Morning. In the distance Sulbha is seen walking past the wall. She comes up to a tree at the foot of which Kamlabai sits sulking.

SULBHA: Er, Kamlabai, please come and see me in the office.
KAMLABAI (*still sulking*): Hmm. (*Sulbha moves away.*)

In the office, Sulbha sits down at the desk. Camera draws back to show Kamlabai walking into the room.

SULBHA: Come in, Kamlabai, I want to ask you something.

A close view of Kamlabai bending forward in front of Sulbha's desk.

KAMLABAI: I don't want to stay here,

A close view of Sulbha.

SULBHA: Do you want to go home?

A close view of Kamlabai.

KAMLABAI: I don't have a home.

Sunanda Hirwe looks up from her typewriter.

KAMLABAI (*off*): She has spoilt my life, the whore!

A close view of Kamlabai.

KAMLABAI: That is my experience.

A close view of Sulbha as she listens to Kamlabai's story.

KAMLABAI (*off*): The whore, she has spoilt her whole life as well.

A close view of Kamlabai. She spits out her words.

KAMLABAI: My own daughter, she made me homeless. When she dies, there'll be no one to put a drop of water in her mouth. Just wait and see—only the flies will gather around her corpse!

Kamlabai in the foreground left. Sulbha faces her on the other side of the table.

SULBHA: Kamlabai, stop it! Aren't you her mother?

Sulbha sits with her back to the camera in the foreground right; Kamlabai stands across the table facing her.

KAMLABAI: Yes. But did she behave like a daughter with me? I struggled so hard to bring her up properly after her father died!

A close view of Kamlabai's face, left of the frame.

KAMLABAI: I was weary of struggling alone, so I remarried. But my daughter, the bitch, she missed school to keep her stepfather company, and threw me out of my home.

Sunanda looks up again from her typewriter.

KAMLABAI (*off*): Why?

Kamlabai's face left of the frame.

KAMLABAI: Because I came between the two of them. I have no home. (*She breaks down and sobs, covering her mouth with the end of her sari.*)

Sulbha sits listening to Kamlabai. She rises and walks round the table to where Kamlabai stands, the camera panning with her.

SULBHA: Hmm. Kamlabai, we shall have to decide about what we can do for you. But till such time I will give you a job to do. You shall keep my office clean, keep my files in order, and keep me informed about my visitors. (*She puts a hand on Kamlabai's shoulder.*) All right?

KAMLABAI: Yes.

SULBHA: Now let me see you smile. (*Kamlabai smiles shyly and wipes her tears.*)

The open door of the office viewed from inside. Chandmal Bhandari, a tradesman, stands smiling at the door.

CHANDMAL: *Namaskar*, Bai. May I come in?

SULBHA (*off*): Yes, come in. (*Kamlabai goes out of the room.*)

Sulbha still stands in front of her desk. She moves back to her chair and sits down. Chandmal comes and sits in front of her with his back to the camera.

SULBHA: Sit down.

View of Chandmal over Sulbha's shoulder. Sunanda can be seen at the back.

CHANDMAL: I am Chandmal Bhandari. I have been supplying saris to the Ashram.

SULBHA: Hmm. Have you brought any quotations?

CHANDMAL (*surprised*): Er, yes.

View of Sulbha over Chandmal's shoulder. She picks up a file and rings the bell on the table.

SULBHA: All right, leave it with me. I'll look into it later.

View over Sulbha's shoulder, Chandmal faces the camera. Sunanda gets up and comes towards the table.

CHANDMAL: It is we who supply the saris to this Ashram—we've been doing it for four years now.

A close view of Sulbha to the right of the frame.

SULBHA: That's all right. We'll be deciding only after we've looked at the other quotations. (*She turns to Sunanda, who is out of the frame.*) Get me Utpala Joshi's file.

CHANDMAL (*off*): Bai——

A close view of Chandmal. In the background, Sunanda goes back to her desk and picks up a file.

CHANDMAL: We are the regular suppliers here. For the last four years every piece of cloth, every sari has come from us.

Camera at the side of Sulbha's table. Sulbha sits on the right. Chandmal is seen on the left. As Sulbha speaks, Sunanda gives her a file and moves away.

SULBHA: I'll go myself and have a look at the saris in the shop, and then think about it. You can go.

CHANDMAL: You will come to the shop? Why not? Do come! It will be a great honour if you visit our humble shop. *Namaskar.*

SULBHA: *Namaskar.* (*Chandmal leaves. Sulbha goes back to work.*)

A film show at the Ashram. In the dark, Sulbha can be seen with her back to the camera, in the foreground right. The projector can be seen running on the left, some distance away. The girls of the Ashram sit on the floor. On the screen is a song sequence from a Hindi hit.*

A series of shots follow, of the film on the screen and members of the audience. On the screen, young lovers gyrate to an absurd love song. The girls watch avidly. Sulbha's smiling face in the dark, comes amidst

Amar, Akbar, Anthony, directed by Manmohan Desai, 1977.

4

shots of the faces of the inmates. The mad girl sits looking at her hands, her writhing fingers moving in convulsive rhythm.

In the dark, a close view of Sulbha, who moves away to the right.

A woman hurries up to Sulbha's office, holding a piece of paper in her hand. It is Utpala. Looking around furtively, she tries to attach the paper to the bolt of the door. Sulbha is seen in the distance, moving towards the office.

> SULBHA: Who is there? (*Utpala turns towards the voice.*) Utpala! (*Sulbha quickens her pace.*)

Utpala in front of the closed office door, looking guilty. Sulbha walks into the frame from the right and takes the piece of paper from Utpala's hand.

> SULBHA: What is this? Come inside. (*She unlocks the door.*)

View from inside the room. The door is pushed open and Sulbha enters. Utpala stands leaning against the door frame. Sulbha advances into the room, reading the note.

> SULBHA: Come in. (*Reading*) Beware! Satyabhama steals vegetables. Rukmini steals soap. The tailoring teacher steals thread. The gatekeeper, Shidore, takes bribes. (*Turning to Utpala.*) Why have you written an anonymous letter, Utpala, huh? Do you know how many complaints have been made to the Chairperson about you?
>
> UTPALA: It must be the gatekeeper, the tailoring teacher and Satyabhamabai who have complained. (*She glares resentfully, then lowers her head when Sulbha does not reply.*)

A close view of Sulbha.

> SULBHA: What wrong have you done to them?

A close view of Utpala, clinging to the door, her eyes flashing with resentment.

> UTPALA: I know all about their misdeeds. That is why they don't want me here.

A close view of Sulbha with her back to the camera. She turns and is seen in profile, moving to the window next to the door as she speaks. Utpala is revealed in the background.

SULBHA: Hmm. What do they do?

A close view of Utpala looking defiant and angry.

UTPALA: They steal Ashram property, and sell them outside.

Sulbha stands near the window. She turns to Utpala as she speaks. She moves closer to Utpala, camera moving with her. Utpala starts sobbing, covering her mouth with her hand.

SULBHA: Still, writing an anonymous letter is an offence, Utpala. To bring somebody else's offence to light, why should you commit a new offence, hmm? Don't cry now. (*She turns to the camera in a close up. Utpala, no longer in the frame, sobs in the background.*) I have to answer on your behalf before the Managing Committee. How old is your child?

A close view of Utpala turning a tear-stained face towards Sulbha, who is out of the frame.

UTPALA: Six months. You're so different from the previous Superintendent, Bai. She used to get all the work done by us. She was removed. (*She whispers her next words.*) Some Ashram girls were discovered at a party thrown by Madan Seth!

A close view of Sulbha in profile, as she turns her face, standing with her back to the camera.

A close view of Utpala against the door.

UTPALA: They say that the Chairmanbai also had a hand in that.

Sulbha in the foreground, facing the camera, turns back towards Utpala, who still stands clutching the door frame, sobbing.

SULBHA: You may go, Utpala. (*Utpala leaves. Sulbha tears up the note.*)

Morning. Inside the office, the gatekeeper stands, his eyes lowered, in the foreground, left, facing Sulbha's desk. Next to him stands the peon. The tailoring teacher, Rukminibai and Satyabhamabai stand facing the camera with their backs to the cupboards lining the wall on the left.

SULBHA: You had better take this as my last warning to you. (*Camera shifts to Sulbha, who rises from her chair as she speaks. She moves past the far end of the desk as the camera draws back again behind the men to show her in front of the desk now.*) From now on I may check the goods in your custody any time. I will not tolerate any erasing or rewriting in the register. All records should be completed every day.

A cluster of curious girls at the office door.

SULBHA (*off*): Understand?

A close view of Sulbha. Camera moves back with her to the other side of the desk where she stands near her chair.

SULBHA: While checking, if I find anything missing, I shall take serious action. And tell the girls that morning prayer is compulsory from tomorrow.

The morning prayer being held in the Ashram courtyard. The girls stand in rows, facing Sunanda Hirwe, who sings a song in praise of God. They all stand with folded hands and the other girls pick up the refrain of Sunanda's song. The attendants stand facing the rows of girls, next to Sunanda. A series of shots show the girls, Sulbha slowly making her way through the rows, Sunanda's face transformed as she sings. There are some latecomers who silently slip into the rows, little incidents of teasing, and close views of some of the girls as they sing. The camera draws back from Sunanda as her voice rises on the last notes of the song. Sulbha now stands next to her. At the end of the song the girls disperse in different directions.

Song: The one who fills the sky with light
And banishes darkness, the merciful one,
O come among us and give us your blessings.
This our sacred home is a reflection of your presence.
In the wind and the stars I have read your name.
All creation, birth and death,
Are expressions of you, O compassionate one.
It is your beauty that is seen in the spring flowers,
Your love the clouds shower on us.
When will I offer my heart to your dancing feet?

A close view of Sulbha, looking towards the girls, who are out of the frame, moving away.

The gatekeeper, in casual clothes, is seen walking away down the courtyard where the prayer meeting was held.

SULBHA (*off*): Gatekeeper! (*He stops on hearing her call.*)

A close view of Sulbha as before.

SULBHA: Please come here.

The gatekeeper walks cautiously back towards Sulbha, who is out of the frame, and stops some distance from the camera.

SULBHA (*off*): Where is your uniform?

A closer view of the gatekeeper, who fingers his sleeveless jacket as he speaks.

GATEKEEPER: I have sent it to the wash.

A close view of Sulbha, looking stern.

SULBHA: Why has it not been washed? Why, huh?

The gatekeeper stands as before, looking sly and guilty.

GATEKEEPER: I had some guests, and my wife was ill, Baisaheb.

A big close up of Sulbha.

SULBHA: You are on duty without your uniform. Aren't you ashamed of yourself?

A big close up of the gatekeeper looking downward.

SULBHA (*off*): Take off that jacket!

A big close up of Sulbha as before.

SULBHA: And go home and put on your uniform!

The gatekeeper reluctantly takes off his jacket. As he turns and walks away, a piece of paper drops on the ground from the jacket. Camera tilts down to the piece of paper.

A close view of Sulbha, who has noticed the paper on the ground and moves to the left of the camera to pick it up.

Sulbha straightens up, holding an envelope in her hand. She reads the letter in the envelope, then, putting it away, looks at the receding figure of the gatekeeper, who is out of the frame.

Night. A large, empty oil drum in the dark. The gatekeeper's stick strikes it twice.

The gatekeeper's face, looking towards the camera. He turns and scans the darkness.

The oil drum stands in the dark. The gatekeeper's stick strikes it twice.

Two girls are seen running across to the right in the distance, between two sets of barracks.

The gatekeeper turns to look towards the camera again.

The faces of Satyabhamabai and Jaswandi appear from behind a wall on the left. They step out, and furtively and swiftly move towards the camera.

View from the top. The two women, with their backs to the camera, run past the outer wall of the Mahilashram, towards the gatekeeper, who stands in a little pool of light.

Satyabhamabai and Jaswandi enter the frame from the left. The gatekeeper stands waiting in the right. He silently gestures to them to wait, then looks around cautiously. He has a torch under his arm, and holds his stick. After making sure that no one is watching, he again gestures to the women, who follow him as he goes to the right.

The large outer gate of the Ashram viewed from inside. The wicket gate opens with a noise. The gatekeeper, Satyabhamabai and Jaswandi enter the Ashram. A light is turned on suddenly, and the three stand frozen in their places, staring out front.

A grim looking Sulbha rises from where she has been sitting. She clears her throat.

SULBHA: Come to the office.

In the dark, a close view of Sulbha's hand holding up Jaswandi's hand which has a ring on one finger. The camera moves up to their faces, then pulls back as Sulbha speaks. The room is Sulbha's office, lit by the lamp on her table.

SULBHA: A present from Madhu Boravke, hmm? (*Camera pans with Sulbha as she moves right to the gatekeeper.*) Got your share of the presents? Did you? (*Camera moves behind Satyabhamabai as Sulbha approaches her.*) I can see it's a new sari. (*She fingers the sari, then jerks away from Satyabhamabai in disgust. She moves past Jaswandi to the left, then turns upon them ferociously.*) Living in this Ashram and indulging in prostitution, don't you feel ashamed of yourselves? (*To Satyabhamabai*) Jaswandi is like a daughter to you. (*She moves to the gatekeeper.*) You shall be punished. I'll teach you a lesson! (*To the peon and Rukminibai who are at the back of the room.*) And you had better take note of what I am saying. (*To the gatekeeper*) Get out of here. (*To Satyabhamabai*) Go away. (*They leave silently. Jaswandi, who is out of the frame, is the only one left. Camera pans as Sulbha moves towards her.*) What punishment shall I give you? (*She moves closer to Jaswandi and speaks with suppressed rage and despair.*) When will you learn? You had to leave home because you were deceived once. After staying for two and a half years in this place, you behave like this again? How many times are you going to be deceived? I cannot punish you. (*She turns away sharply to the left, camera closing in on her alone.*) Go!

Day. In the office, Sulbha dials a number on her telephone.

SULBHA: Hello!

Sheila Samson in her drawing room. Paintings on the wall, potted plants and ornamental cushions, all display opulence, as does Mrs Samson's expensive attire.

MRS SAMSON (*on the phone*): Sheila Samson here.

Sulbha at her desk.

SULBHA: This is Sulbha Mahajan speaking.

Sheila Samson in her drawing room.

MRS SAMSON: Ah. Tell me quickly. I have to go out for lunch.

Sulbha at her desk, speaking briskly.

SULBHA: Madam, one of the girls here, Jaswandi, is having an affair with a man outside the Ashram. I got to know about it only last night.

A close view of Sunanda Hirwe who looks up.

SULBHA (*off*): And . . .

A big close up of Sulbha, left of the frame.

SULBHA: . . . the gatekeeper and the woman in charge of the kitchen have been helping her. Oh yes, I have proof. And, Madam, they have both been paid for their help.

A close view of Mrs Samson, who speaks briskly.

MRS SAMSON: Take away whatever they have received, and fine them ten rupees each. And give them a warning. Put the girl in a lock-up for two days, without food. Anything else?

Sulbha in a big close up. She looks surprised and unhappy about Mrs Samson's quick solutions.

SULBHA: That's all.

Mrs Samson in a big close up to the right of the frame.

MRS SAMSON: From now on, don't ring me up before nine at night. Good-bye. (*She puts the receiver back impatiently.*)

Sulbha looks disappointed. She puts the receiver down slowly, pre-occupied with her thoughts. She leans back as the music swells and the camera draws into a big close up.

Through the bars of the Ashram lock-up, Sulbha is seen walking down the path past the wall. As she nears the lock-up, the camera draws back suddenly to reveal Jaswandi standing near the barred window, watching her approach. Sulbha notices her and stops, then bows her head and goes right, past the lock-up. The camera pans to Jaswandi, who moves to another window to watch the receding figure of Sulbha.

A view of the Ashram girls sitting on the ground. Utpala sits with her baby on her lap.

A close view of Sulbha sitting under a tree. Rukminibai stands near her. The camera draws back over the heads of a large group of girls who sit listening to her.

> SULBHA: It was wrong of Jaswandi to try to run away from the Ashram. If you run away in this manner, you'll only be brought back here again. Is that . . .

Another group of girls facing the camera.

> SULBHA (*off*): . . . what you want? Instead, if we try to understand each other, discuss your problems, your sorrows . . .

A close view of Sulbha, desperately trying to establish some communication with the girls.

> SULBHA: . . . then together we can find some way out. Hmm?

Another section of the girls, with Kamlabai on the right.

Sulbha seen over Farida's bent head. Farida has her back to the camera.

> SULBHA: Farida—Farida! You tell us, how did you get here? (*Farida lifts her head.*)

A section of the girls with Farida in the centre. The conversation between Sulbha and Farida is carried on in Hindi.

> FARIDA: The usual way. My husband threw me out of the house.

A close view of Sulbha, right of the frame.

> SULBHA: You don't have any children, do you?

A close view of Farida, left of the frame.

> FARIDA: No, sister. I was the fourth wife of my husband. My hair was thick and long.

A big close up of one of the girls, listening to Farida's story.

Farida's face, left of the frame.

> FARIDA: My husband said, 'Your hair drives men mad. You are not
> a well-behaved girl.'

A close view of Sulbha, listening to Farida's story.

> FARIDA (*off*): He started beating me.

Farida's face as before.

> FARIDA: I took a lot of beating. He cut off all my hair, sister! Then,
> when he started trying to kill me, I ran away from home.

A close view of Sulbha.

> SULBHA: Hmm. If I write to your parents, would you go back
> to them?

Farida in the midst of other girls. Camera draws close to her as she
speaks.

> FARIDA: They are poor. They have many children, sister. My father
> said, 'For us, you are dead. Go and jump into a well.'

A big close up of another girl, Mangala, as she listens to Farida's
story.

Farida's face in a close up.

> FARIDA: This is my home now.

A close view of Sulbha, who sighs and leans back, turning to another girl.

> SULBHA: Champa, you are from Solapur, aren't you?

A section of the girls with Champa in the centre. She is evidently in
an advanced state of pregnancy. Camera closes in on her as she speaks.

> CHAMPA: Yes, Bai. I am from Sanghvi. I am of a low caste. My
> husband died of tuberculosis, leaving an eight-year-old son to
> feed. I had to become a labourer.

A big close up of Kamlabai as she listens to Champa's story.

   CHAMPA (*off*): I used to work on Manikrao Yadav's farm.

A close view of Sulbha.

   CHAMPA (*off*): Rehman was the driver of his truck.

The farm where Champa used to work. Near a stack of hay, under a tree, Champa moves closer to Rehman as the camera draws back. They are both sitting on the grass. Rehman speaks in Hindi.

   CHAMPA: I get very little wages, Rehman. It's difficult to manage. Will you lend me some money?

   REHMAN (*stroking her arm and shoulder*): It's time for the elections in the factory. The owner wants women. He wants to give a drinks party. Thirty rupees each time. It's dirty work, but you'll get money. Shall I tell the boss?

Champa turns to look at him, then turns away and looks downwards. Rehman pushes her down on the hay, and turns to her.

In front of Champa's hovel, an old man sits with a young boy standing near him. Champa approaches them from the back, gives some clothes to the boy and caresses him. Then she hands some clothes to the old man. The camera pans as she goes left to enter the shack. An older woman sits washing vessels. Champa shows her two saris before entering the shack.

A close view of a large grinding stone. Camera draws back to show Champa grinding grain. She stops, puts her hand on her forehead, then rises quickly as she starts retching.

A close view of Champa lying on the ground inside a shack, groaning with pain.

A close view of the impassive face of the woman who is the abortionist.

   WOMAN: Keep quiet!

Another close view of Champa, who groans loudly.

The woman looks up towards the right.

View from inside the shack. The makeshift door is removed from outside, and a policeman appears.

POLICEMAN: Hey! You are trying to do an abortion! Come to the police station!

A big close up of Champa.

CHAMPA: And with the fruit of my sin growing in my belly . . .

A close view of Sulbha.

CHAMPA (*off*) : . . . I came here.

A bell rings. Sulbha looks at her watch, then rises.

SULBHA: Go on. Go for your lunch.

Mangala, very young and pregnant, walks on the open verandah in front of the well. Camera pans to show her stopping at a wooden pillar as she calls out to Sulbha, who is seen in the distance.

MANGALA: Bai!

Sulbha, who was about to step off the veranda, stops and turns to Mangala. She walks up to the girl where she stands, taking off her glasses. Camera moves closer to them.

MANGALA: *Namaste*, Bai.
SULBHA (*smiles*) : *Namaste*.
MANGALA (*offering Sulbha some flowers*) : Bai, you love flowers, don't you? That's why I brought them.
SULBHA: They are beautiful. (*Affectionately*) How do you feel?
MANGALA: Bai, something keeps moving in my stomach!
SULBHA: That happens. (*They both laugh happily.*)
MANGALA (*as Sulbha puts a flower in Mangala's hair*) : Bai, how many children do you have?
SULBHA: I have one daughter.
MANGALA: What is her name?
SULBHA: Rani.
MANGALA: Do you have her photograph with you?
SULBHA: Yes, I have.
MANGALA: Will you show it to me?
SULBHA (*touching Mangala's hair affectionately*) : Come, I'll show you. (*They move away to the left.*)

Sulbha and Mangala enter Sulbha's bedroom, Sulbha talking about her childhood. She puts the files in her hand on the desk and sits down on the chair next to it. Mangala stands with her back to the cupboard near the door.

SULBHA: . . . and two long braids like you. At school they used to call me a clown. (*They laugh together.*)

MANGALA: How can that be, Bai?

SULBHA: It's true! (*She laughs.*)

MANGALA: You don't look like a clown. (*She laughs.*)

SULBHA: Come, you wanted to see my home, didn't you? (*She breathes a happy sigh as she brings out an album from a drawer. Mangala leans forward.*)

View from the other side of the table. Mangala leans forward on the table on the left. Sulbha puts on her glasses. They smile happily at the photographs.

SULBHA: Look! This is our home. This is Rani. Here's Rani's father. Here are her uncle, her aunty and her grandmother.

A close view of a stack of new saris in Chandmal's store. Chandmal's hand rests on the saris, with rings on the fingers. As he speaks, camera pulls back to show Chandmal on the right and Sulbha at the back on the left, facing the camera.

CHANDMAL: Let us now decide about the price.

SULBHA (*looking at the saris kept in front of her*): Do you have some more of this type? (*A man brings another stack of saris.*)

CHANDMAL: You are giving the matter too much thought, Bai. So many people make money out of the Ashram. Why should you object to my making a little money too? It's not your own money anyway.

SULBHA (*giving him a sharp glance*): Sethji, you should give us a discount as it is a public institution. Show me some more.

CHANDMAL (*giving her an envelope*): Bai, take this. A little gift.

SULBHA (*looking suspiciously at the envelope*): What?

CHANDMAL: Take a look. (*She looks into the envelope.*)

SULBHA (*shocked at being offered a bribe*): Why should I misuse the Ashram's funds? (*She throws the envelope on the ground with a gesture of disgust and rushes out of the shop, Chandmal's laughter following her as the camera pans away from him.*)

A baby in a cradle. The Ashram girls crowd around as Sulbha bends over it happily. It is Champa's baby boy. Camera draws back in a top shot. There are more girls sitting on the floor. The occasion is the ceremony of providing the baby with a name.

> SULBHA: Hmm, aha! What a pretty child, Champa! What name will you give him?
> GIRLS: Bai, you tell us.
> SULBHA: No, no, I won't. You must decide on the name. Come on, suggest some names.
> GIRLS: Amitabh!—No, Dharmendra!
> SULBHA: What is this? Can't you suggest any name other than those of film stars?
> GIRLS: Why don't you tell us, Bai?
> SULBHA: Shall I? (*She bends down, as if to confer with the baby. Then rises triumphantly with the name.*) Subhash!

She laughs happily with the girls as the name is accepted without opposition. In the midst of all the laughter and merriment, the mad girl sits musing on the window sill in the background.

A view of the girls on the floor, laughing, facing the camera.

A view of the happy crowd near the cradle.

Camera pulls away from a top shot of a group of girls running between the barracks, looking upwards. It pans to look at a larger group of girls, with Satyabhamabai and the tailoring teacher in front, waving frantically and shouting, looking upwards. At the back of the group, more girls come running.

View from the top. The peon, Rukminibai, the gatekeeper and Sulbha rush down from an open veranda near where the crowd has collected. The camera pulls back over the shoulders of the mad girl, who is standing on the roof of one of the buildings, unaware of the commotion below, watching her writhing fingers. Sulbha and her companions make their way through the crowd, and appear before the building.

Above the raised hands of the crowd, the camera looks at the mad girl standing precariously at the edge of the roof, wringing her hands.

MAD GIRL: Kill him! Black snake! Poisonous snake! He is licking my body!

View of the agitated crowd below. Camera moves to the left, to where Sulbha stands with Rukminibai and Satyabhamabai. The peon and the gatekeeper stand near them. Sulbha tries to stop the girls from shouting, but her own voice is drowned in the noise.

VOICES: Come down! Come down!

SULBHA: Girls, keep quiet! Silence!

MAD GIRL: Always after me——

The mad girl on the roof brushes off the imaginary snake in a frenzy.

MAD GIRL: He is coming, coming on my legs!

A close view of Sulbha watching the mad girl.

The mad girl on the roof, battling with her fantasies.

MAD GIRL: He's coming! He's coming! Kill him!

Sunanda and Jangam stand in front of the crowd. Sunanda draws closer to Jangam as they watch the mad girl, who is out of the frame.

Sulbha seen with the attendants and the peon and the gatekeeper.

SULBHA (*to the girls who keep shouting*): Hey, please wait a bit. (*To the gatekeeper and the peon*) You just do this. Approach from behind, catch her and bring her down. But be careful. Go on. Hurry. Go. (*The gatekeeper and the peon move away to the right.*)

The mad girl brushes the ground in front of her as she screams.

MAD GIRL: He's coming! Kill him!

In the distance, the peon and the gatekeeper are seen carrying the ladder, walking up to a building on the left of the frame. They place the ladder against the wall of the building.

The mad girl rises and stares to the right.

The crowd below, with the tailoring teacher, Utpala, Jaswandi and others behind them, all looking upwards.

View from the ground where the peon holds the ladder as the gate-keeper climbs to the roof.

Another view of the crowd from further away.

View from below. The gatekeeper gets off the ladder onto the ledge.

The mad girl brushes the imaginary snake off her clothes.

A close view of Sulbha watching the mad girl.

The gatekeeper is seen hauling himself up on the stretch of the roof behind the mad girl. The camera moves with him as he cautiously steps towards the girl. She turns towards him, but does not see him and turns away again, immersed in her fantasy. The gatekeeper catches her by the shoulders. The camera pulls sharply away over the heads of the crowd. In the distance, the gatekeeper is seen escorting the mad girl away from the roof. The girls below rush towards the building where the drama took place. The camera closes in on Sulbha and Rukminibai.

> SULBHA: Rukminibai, telephone the hospital and ask for the ambulance. (*She remains standing with her back to the camera, as Rukminibai moves away to the right.*)

Night. Sulbha's bedroom. A close view of Sulbha writing a letter to Subhash. The camera moves back slowly to show her writing by the light of a table lamp. She stops to read the letter. She does not read aloud. But her voice is heard over the sound-track.

> SULBHA'S VOICE: Dear Subhash, I decided to sit down and write a letter to you today, come what may. Here everything is fine. I too am happy. How is Rani? Give her my love. (*She starts writing again.*)

A close view of Sulbha. She looks up from her writing and starts sobbing. She takes off her glasses, turns her face towards the camera, leans her head on her arm and weeps.

Day. A room in the Ashram with a large table on which stands a jug of water. There are also coasters with glasses, paper and files. The

Sulbha in the opening shot—dozing, waiting. [p. 1]

At the women's home—the girls in a queue spot Sulbha. [p. 28]

Time for the weekly rations. [p. 28]

Sulbha extricates herself from the grip of the mad girl. [p. 35]

Sulbha, in her room in the night, reading and thinking. [p. 36]

Watching the mad girl on the parapet above, with terror. [p. 52]

In the same scene, Sulbha tries to stop the girls from shouting. [p. 53]

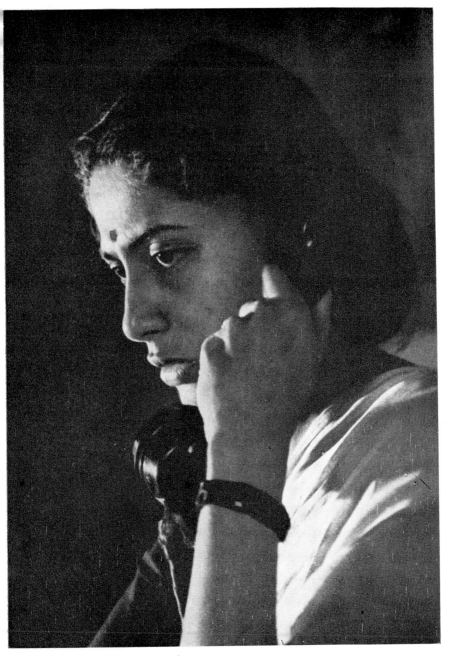

A late night call from the lecherous MLA. [p. 63]

Subhash at the women's home, rudely checked at the gate, till
Sulbha comes out to receive him. [p. 68]

Bakula and Gulab are brought back to the women's home by the police. [p. 90]

Bakula and Gulab in the lock-up, resentful. [p. 92]

Bakula and Gulab, defiant. [p. 92]

Sulbha faces the one-man commission: 'I decided to change all this.' [p. 100]

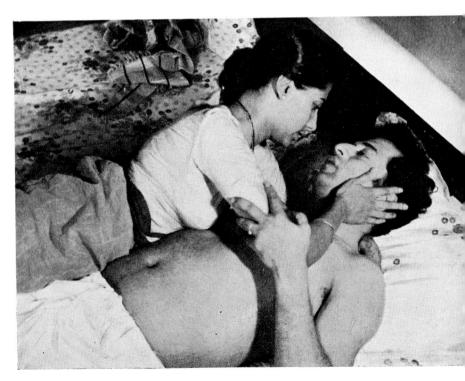

Back home, in bed, Sulbha with Subhash, just before Subhash's 'revelation'. [p. 107]

Managing Committee is in session. Sheila Samson sits at the head of the table on the left. On her right sits Sulbha, facing the camera, and on her left two men with their backs to the camera.

MRS SAMSON: This is the new Superintendent of our Ashram, Mrs Sulbha Mahajan.

SULBHA: *Namaskar.*

MRS SAMSON: She is a gold medallist from the Tata Institute.

Another view of the group. Sulbha in the foreground left, with her back to the camera. Mrs Samson on the right. The first member to be introduced to Sulbha sits opposite her, facing the camera.

MRS SAMSON: I will introduce you to the members of the Managing Committee as this is your first meeting. This is Mr Tirodkar. He is a journalist and runs a weekly. (*Tirodkar, a man with a face like a ferret, smiles and nods. The camera moves left as the introduction proceeds. The men fold their hands in greeting.*) Mr Vadimbe is the Headmaster of our girls' school. He is also a social worker. (*Vadimbe is a plump, baby-faced man with a little cropped moustache just under his nose.*) Mr Baba Badkas is a retired pleader and for many years a member of our Ashram Committee. (*Badkas is a gaunt, doddering old man who is hard of hearing.*)

On the other side of the table, next to Sulbha, sit two other women, both plump and matronly. The camera moves from left to right, keeping the men's heads in the foreground, out of focus.

MRS SAMSON (*off*): This is Mrs Anandibai Navare, a writer. (*She looks to her left and smiles.*) And this is Mrs Shakuntalabai Sawant, the wife of an ex-MLA. (*Shakuntalabai bends her head and lifts her knitting needles in response.*)

A view of Mrs Samson's side of the table.

MRS SAMSON: Shall we start, Mrs Mahajan?

SULBHA: Yes.

MRS SAMSON: We are already late. Is there anyone else coming?

SULBHA: The Collector, the Officer in charge of Social Welfare and the DSP have informed us of their inability to attend due to pressing work.

Tirodkar turns to Vadimbe.

5

TIRODKAR: As usual, eh Vadimbe? (*He laughs. Vadimbe laughs with him, making a neighing sound.*)

Mrs Samson rings a bell to summon the first case before the Committee.

MRS SAMSON: Send in the first case.

The door of the room viewed from inside. Subhadra enters carrying her baby, looking suspiciously around. The camera pans with her, then draws back as she moves forward to stand between Mrs Samson and Sulbha. Now the whole length of the table is in view, with a flower vase at the end near the camera.

MRS SAMSON: What is her name?
SULBHA: Subhadra Ramprasad.
SUBHADRA (*defiantly*): No. I am Subhadra Shivcharan. (*She speaks in Hindi.*)

Tirodkar cracks another joke and looks at Vadimbe.

TIRODKAR: Is there a stay order on the name Ramprasad? (*Vadimbe laughs with Tirodkar.*)

Sulbha looks at the two men, who are out of the frame. They can be heard laughing even as she speaks.

SULBHA: Ramprasad is her husband. She does not wish to . . .

A close view of Vadimbe.

SULBHA (*off*): . . . use his name.
VADIMBE (*sarcastic*): Pride!

A close view of Mrs Samson.

MRS SAMSON: Adultery?

A close view of Mrs Navare.

MRS NAVARE: We can describe her as a wife who is a fallen woman, can't we?

Tirodkar laughs and looks around.

On the sound of Tirodkar's laughter comes a view of Badkas and Vadimbe.

BADKAS: What does she say?

VADIMBE (*loudly*): She doesn't want to take her husband's name.

BADKAS (*shocked*): Oh!

A view of the entire table. Except for Sulbha and Subhadra, everybody finds the incident extremely funny. Mrs Sawant continues with her knitting. Camera moves left towards the head of the table, as Sulbha starts reading the case history.

MRS SAMSON: Read the case history.

SULBHA (*reading*): Subhadra Ramprasad. Belongs to Bihar. The second wife of an old man, who already has two grown-up children. After her marriage she ran away with young Shivcharan. Both the father and the husband lodged a complaint. So the police arrested the couple, and there was a case against Shivcharan. That was when the police brought Subhadra to the Ashram. She was pregnant when she came here. Now she has a daughter who is six months old.

A closer view of Mrs Samson and Subhadra.

MRS SAMSON: She must go to her husband. There is no alternative.

SUBHADRA: No! I won't go! I hate him!

MRS SAMSON (*turning to Subhadra*): Why?

SUBHADRA: He is not fit to be my husband. He is old!

Mrs Navare and Mrs Sawant at their end of the table.

SUBHADRA (*off*): He is dirty!

MRS SAWANT (*lifting her eyes from her knitting, speaks mildly*): He is old, is he?

MRS NAVARE (*dreamily*): It reminds me of Deval's play, *Sharada*.

A view of Mrs Samson, Subhadra and Sulbha.

MRS SAMSON: Is her husband ready to take her back with her daughter?

SUBHADRA (*to Mrs Samson*): Even if he is, I shall not go.

A close view of Vadimbe holding a transistor to his ear as he listens intently to the cricket commentary.

SUBHADRA (*off*) : I will never go and live with that ape!
MRS SAMSON (*off, angrily*) : Then who will you live with?

Mrs Samson, Sulbha and Subhadra at the head of the table.

SUBHADRA: Baisaheb has written a letter to Nagpur. Shivcharan will come and fetch me.
MRS SAMSON (*to Sulbha*) : What is she talking about?

A big close up of Sulbha looking uncomfortable.

SULBHA: Oh yes. I had written to the Inspector of Police in Nagpur, but it is only today that I got a reply. Shivcharan has taken another wife.

Subhadra's ravaged face looking at Sulbha.

SUBHADRA: What do you mean?

A close view of Mrs Samson looking up at Subhadra.

MRS SAMSON (*in Hindi*): Subhadra, Shivcharan has married some other woman.

A close view of Subhadra, who refuses to believe what she has just heard.

SUBHADRA: No! It cannot be! It cannot be!

Mrs Samson briskly gives her verdict, then rings the bell for the next case.

MRS SAMSON: She must go back to her husband. Send a letter asking him to come here. Next case.

Vadimbe stops listening to the transistor and leans towards Tirodkar.

VADIMBE: Gavaskar was bowled out at 98!
TIRODKAR: Huh! Hopeless.
VADIMBE: Hmm. Quite right. (*He puts the transistor back against his ear.*)

Subhadra stands in a state of shock. Sulbha looks at her.

SULBHA: Subhadra, go to your room.
SUBHADRA: No! This is not possible! (*Sulbha rises and goes to her.*)

SULBHA: Subhadra, go to your room.

SUBHADRA: No!

View from the other end of the table. As Sulbha tries to coax Subhadra to leave the room, all the Committee members start talking among themselves.

SULBHA: Subhadra, listen to me please. I will come to you right soon.

BADKAS: Come on now, take the next case.

SULBHA (*trying to gently push Subhadra out of the room*): Subhadra, I'll talk to Madam.

SUBHADRA (*going to Mrs Samson*): Baiji, you do something, Baiji! Baiji, I don't want to go there! (*The camera moves from behind the men on the left, up to the head of the table.*)

MRS SAMSON (*paying no attention to the frantic cries of Subhadra*): I want to finish the meeting early. I have to be at the dog show at the Rotary Club.

SULBHA (*holding the struggling Subhadra*): Rukminibai!

SUBHADRA (*to Sulbha*): Baiji, you say something! Baiji, I don't want to go!

SULBHA: Subhadra, don't behave like this.

SUBHADRA (*getting violent*): Leave me alone! I shall take revenge! I shall take revenge! I won't go to him! I won't go to him!

Rukminibai manages to take Subhadra out of the room. Camera follows them to the door where Sulbha turns to look at the Committee members, who are now out of the frame. But on the soundtrack there is a murmur of happy conversation. Camera moves with Sulbha as she approaches the table, sits down, and clears her throat.

SULBHA (*to Mrs Samson*): The next case is of an unmarried mother, Utpala Joshi.

Mrs Samson looks at the papers in front of her.

MRS SAMSON: Yes. She is to be rehabilitated. There are many complaints about her from the staff here.

A close view of Mrs Sawant counting the stitches on her needle.

Utpala, carrying her child, enters by the door. The camera draws back as she approaches Mrs Samson. Sulbha puts on her glasses. As she reads from her file, the camera moves behind the men, towards the other end of the table.

SULBHA: She is the daughter of a middle-class doctor. Her daughter is eight months old. The child was born in the Ashram. Her father is ready to accept her, but on one condition, that she does not take her child with her. For this he has also sent five hundred rupees.

MRS SAMSON: Send her back to her father. We shall put her daughter in an orphanage. (*Looking at the others.*) All right?

TIRODKAR (*nods*): Yes.

MRS NAVARE: Yes, fine. (*Looks at Mrs Sawant for support.*)

SULBHA: But she is not prepared to part with her child.

TIRODKAR: Not prepared? But why?

Sulbha takes off her glasses to reply to Tirodkar.

SULBHA: If she wants to stand on her own feet, we should give her a chance to prove herself. Till she gets a job, the Ashram can remain responsible for her . . .

Mrs Samson, holding up her compact mirror, stops in the middle of touching up her lips to respond sharply to Sulbha's suggestion.

SULBHA (*off*): . . . if no one has any objections.

MRS SAMSON: Mrs Mahajan, do you have any idea about the finances of the Ashram? It is impossible for us to feed and clothe people who can be accommodated elsewhere.

A close view of Vadimbe, who removes the transistor from his ear to speak to Utpala.

VADIMBE: Look, Miss Utpala Joshi. We quite understand your motherly emotions.

Badkas puts a hand behind his ear in an effort to hear what is going on.

VADIMBE (*off*): But this child of yours is a fruit of your sin.

Vadimbe speaks with a condescending smile, as if to a difficult child.

VADIMBE: It should be got rid of. Otherwise society won't accept you. Hmm? Later on you might even get married. Isn't that so?

Utpala looks resolute.

UTPALA: I won't leave my daughter. Nor will I go back to my father.

A view of Mrs Navare and Mrs Sawant.

MRS NAVARE: Then send the child to her father, whoever that is.

MRS SAWANT: Why should he accept the child?

Utpala stands between Mrs Samson and Sulbha.

UTPALA: I am ready to leave the Ashram with my child. Allow me to go.

MRS SAMSON: All right. You put it in writing that you are leaving the Ashram of your own free will. That would be best. Mrs Mahajan, hand over to her the five hundred rupees that her father has sent. It'll come of use. On behalf of the Ashram, give her a sari and a blouse.

UTPALA: I don't want anything. I only want my daughter. I'm going, Bai. (*She leaves.*)

View from the other end of the table.

MRS SAMSON: Come on. It's 5.30. We must disperse. (*To Sulbha*) Send my transport allowance across to me. (*They all rise to leave.*)

VADIMBE (*shouting at the sleeping Badkas*): The meeting is over! They are paying the transport allowance! Come on!

BADKAS (*waking up suddenly*): I too must go to the eye specialist. For a cataract operation.

VADIMBE: And I have to take out a women's procession against pornographic films! (*They file past Sulbha. Camera closes in on her as she silently watches them leave.*)

The open veranda outside the room. In the foreground right, Subhadra sits on the veranda with her baby, leaning against a wooden pillar. Sulbha appears from the left, walking towards her with her head bowed. Subhadra rises as Sulbha comes closer.

SUBHADRA: Bai, do I really have to go back to that worthless man? Has Shivcharan really got married?

SULBHA (*stopping and putting a comforting hand on Subhadra's arm*): Yes, Subhadra. (*Subhadra moves away silently, leaving Sulbha staring*

*after her. Camera closes in on her unhappy face. She looks at the files in
her hand, then moves away to the right.*)

Night. In the light of her table lamp in the office, Sulbha tries to
put through a long-distance call to her home. The line is disturbed.

SULBHA: Hullo! Hullo! Operator! Yes, put the line through! Hullo
Maya! Yes, this is Sulbha speaking! I've been trying for the last
five or six days, they put me through today! Hullo! (*She hits
and shakes the telephone in an effort to get a clearer connexion.*)

A close view of Sulbha on the left of the frame, shouting to get herself
heard.

SULBHA: Hullo, Maya! Where is Rani? On a trip to where?
Mahabaleswar? Hullo! And where is he? When will he come
back from Delhi? Huh?

Kamlabai sits on the steps outside the office, waiting for her to finish.

SULBHA (*off*): What did you say? Huh?

Sulbha sits at her table in the light of the lamp, struggling with the
phone.

SULBHA: Yes, when will he come? And how are you? Mother-in-
law——— Hullo——— Hullo! Maya! Tell Rani—I am all right!
Tell Rani——— (*The line is disconnected. Disappointed and depressed,
she puts the receiver back on the cradle. Camera moves closer to her face
as she breaks into sobs. The telephone rings again. She hastily picks it up,
wiping her eyes.*) Hullo! (*Her voice is still hoarse.*) Hullo!

A close view of Sulbha, right of the frame.

SULBHA: Mahilashram.

A man sits on a richly decorated divan in a room, talking on the
telephone. He speaks in a drawling voice and in a familiar tone.
Beside him an ornate wood carving rests against the wall on a table,
along with a glass topped table lamp. The man holds a cigarette.

MAN: What's the matter, Bai? I couldn't get your line.

Sulbha in a close view as before.

SULBHA (*surprised*): Mahilashram. Who is speaking?

The man on the divan lets out a cloud of smoke that drifts past the lamp.

MAN: Is it the new Bai?

Sulbha in a close view as before.

SULBHA: Which new Bai?

The man on the divan gives an indulgent smile.

MAN (*deliberately distorting the pronunciation*): Supper-inn-tenddent!

Sulbha speaks on the phone.

SULBHA: Yes, speaking. Who are you?

A closer view of the man and the wood carving.

MAN: I am Bane. (*In English*) Bane MLA speaking. Can you hear me? Hey Bai, I've sent the car. Send a nice looking girl. What? I'll send her back early in the morning. All right?

Sulbha replaces the receiver hastily. Then quickly removes her hand from it as it rings again, staring at it in horror. She rises from the chair, feeling physically ill, with a hand at her throat. She moves away from the table without taking her eyes off the ringing telephone. She puts out the lamp and calls Kamlabai.

SULBHA: Kamlabai, close the office.
KAMLABAI (*off*): What did you say, Bai? (*The telephone keeps ringing in the dark.*)
SULBHA (*releasing all her tension by shouting at Kamlabai*): Close the office! (*She rushes off to the left.*)

A car leaves the porch of the Mahilashram. The gate can be seen behind. In the car sit some men, all wearing the typical politician's white cap. But there is no girl with them.

View from inside. Sulbha opens the door and enters her quarters, then quickly shuts the door, looking frightened.

She comes into the bedroom, slowly advances towards the head of the bed, sits down, turns off the lamp, and lies down in the dark.

Sulbha's quarters from outside. In the darkness a faint light can be seen through the passage window. The door opens and Sulbha comes out in a shaft of light, standing silhouetted against it as she looks around. She comes nearer the camera and a light falls on her face, and the shadows of the crossed bars of the passage window cover her body.

SULBHA: Gatekeeper!

View from the top. Sulbha can be seen far away, walking, running, looking for something in the echoing emptiness of the Ashram grounds.

SULBHA: Gatekeeper!

View from inside a room. Through the bars of a window, Sulbha can be seen looking into the room as she goes left. Camera moves left to the door of the room, which is opened by Sulbha.

The dormitory. Dark and empty. Sulbha enters by a door on the right.

SULBHA: Subhadra! Champa! Mangala! (*Her voice echoes in the large empty space.*)

She runs towards a door, away from the camera, where a red glow can be seen.

A length of open veranda. Sulbha appears at the far end, and runs forward towards the camera.

The empty kitchen bathed in a fiery glow. The door opens from outside and Sulbha comes in. In front of her, a large vessel is on the fire.

A close view of Sulbha's frightened face. She is sweating with fear.

Sulbha's view of the empty room in the eerie red glow.

A close view of Sulbha as before. She looks cautiously towards her right.

A close view of the vessel with something like milk boiling in it.

Sulbha draws back, panting with fear.

View from inside the barracks. In the darkness outside, Sulbha's face can be seen as she moves to the right, looking into the rooms all the time. There is a faint light on her face as she goes past the crossed bars of the windows.

Sulbha runs towards the camera. She leans against a wall on the left, panting, looking around with fear in her eyes. She turns past the wall and goes left, breaking into a run.

Sulbha runs towards the camera as it draws back.

The tortured face of Sulbha as she runs towards the camera.

Sulbha runs down the empty courtyard to the left.

Sulbha's face distorted with fear.

Sulbha's view of the outside gates. They are closing slowly.

Sulbha pants loudly as she runs towards the gates.

The gates closing slowly.

View from outside. Between the closing doors, Sulbha can be seen running.

   SULBHA: Open it! (*It is a desperate cry.*)

From far away the doors are seen closing just as Sulbha reaches them.

   SULBHA: Open it! (*She beats her fists on the closed gates.*)

A close view of Sulbha's hands beating on the wooden gates. The hands slowly slide down as her sobs grow louder. The camera moves to her sweating, weeping face against the door. She turns in a shaft of light towards the camera.

   SULBHA: Open it! Open! Open! Open the door!

A sound of knocking, growing louder.

Through the bars of her window, Sulbha is seen sitting up on her bed with a start, and a loud gasp. Her nightmare is over, but the knocking is real. She gets off the bed in the dark.

Kamlabai stands outside Sulbha's door. The door suddenly opens from inside, and Sulbha appears, looking dishevelled. She is still in the grip of her nightmare.

> KAMLABAI (*urgently*) : Bai!

Kamlabai is seen over the shoulder of Sulbha.

> KAMLABAI: Bai. Come and see what Subhadra has done!

A close view of Sulbha looking dazed.

> SULBHA: Huh?
> KAMLABAI (*off*): Bai, come along. Hurry up, Bai! (*Sulbha moves forward.*)

Sulbha and other women run into the frame, come towards the camera, then Sulbha lets out a shriek of fear and steps back. Camera moves away to show Sulbha's view of Subhadra with her dead child, sitting on the ground, staring in front of her.

Sulbha and Kamlabai stand frozen with shock. In the foreground right, Subhadra sits with her back to the camera. Sulbha comes forward, followed by the other women. She looks at the mangled baby, which is out of the frame on the ground, then moves towards Subhadra.

The faces of Sulbha and Subhadra in profile. Sulbha squats on the left, facing Subhadra. In the faint light, only the outline of their faces can be seen.

> SULBHA: Subhadra, Subhadra, what have you done! (*She shakes Subhadra's still form.*)
> SUBHADRA (*in a lifeless voice*) : I have killed my baby, Baiji.

A close view of Subhadra to the right of the frame. There are no tears in her large eyes.

> SUBHADRA: Baiji, now I won't have to go back to my husband, will I?

A close view of Sulbha, left of the frame, looking at Subhadra in horror.

A close view of Subhadra as before.

SUBHADRA: Now you'll have to send me to jail.

Sulbha stares at Subhadra in silence.

Subhash's car comes down the road outside the Mahilashram and stops near the porch. Subhash comes out carrying a small suitcase, and shuts the door of the car. He puts down the suitcase on the ground, takes out a handkerchief, and moves towards the gate with the suitcase in hand, wiping the sweat off his face. The wicket gate stands open.

View from inside the Ashram. Subhash's feet are seen approaching the wicket gate. He bends and calls out.

SUBHASH: Anybody inside?

Subhash's view of the gatekeeper, who sits at the table in front of the wicket gate.

GATEKEEPER (*rising*): Who is it? What do you want?

The camera draws back outside, as Subhash straightens up and moves left to let the gatekeeper come out.

SUBHASH: *Namaskar.*

GATEKEEPER: (*still suspicious*): *Ram Ram.*

SUBHASH: Will you please open the gate? I want to take the car inside.

GATEKEEPER: No, no! Except for the Chairmanbai's, no one else's car is allowed inside. Those are the orders!

SUBHASH: Are they? (*He tries to go in by the wicket gate but the gatekeeper stops him.*)

GATEKEEPER: Hey, wait! Without filling in the register you can't go inside! (*He goes in, fetches the register and hands it to Subhash.*) Take this. Your name, address, and whom you want to meet.

SUBHASH (*looking annoyed as he fills in the register*): Tell the Bai that Subhash has come.

GATEKEEPER: Whatever that may be, you write it down. Without filling in the register, even God can't enter this place. These are

the orders of the Baisaheb. Wait! (*He takes the register and goes in.*)
Subhash picks up the suitcase, which he had put down near the
wicket gate, takes out cigarettes from his pocket, and moves towards
the car.

Inside the Ashram, Sulbha seen running up all the way to the gate,
smiling.

Subhash stands near the car, lights his cigarette and looks up.

The big gates of the Ashram seen from outside. Sulbha comes out
running through the open wicket gate. Camera pulls away to reveal
Subhash near the car.

SULBHA: Subhash!
SUBHASH (*turning to her with a smile*): Hi!

Subhash stands near the car. Sulbha appears from the right.

SULBHA (*excited and happy*): Subhash, you? So suddenly? You didn't
write, didn't telephone——
SUBHASH: I wanted to give you a surprise. But I had to wait near
the gate like a destitute woman instead.

Another view of Subhash and Sulbha near the car. They are not at
ease with each other.

SULBHA: I am sorry. But I was a little busy.
SUBHASH: It's all right.
SULBHA: And I did not look at the register. How would I know that
you would come so suddenly?

Subhash pulls at his cigarette. They both feel self-conscious and at a
loss for words. Finally they both think of something to say at the same
time. But Subhash does not continue, instead he answers Sulbha's
question.

SULBHA: Rani didn't come?
SUBHASH: She had her examinations.
SULBHA: She is all right, isn't she?
SUBHASH: She is fine. No, no, really!
SULBHA: Come, why don't you come inside?
SUBHASH: Can I take the car in?

SULBHA: Yes, you can.

SUBHASH: Sure?

SULBHA: Quite sure.

SUBHASH (*inviting her to come into the car*): Then, come on.

SULBHA: No, I'll walk. You come in the car. (*Subhash gets into the car. Sulbha takes the suitcase and goes away to the right.*)

Camera pulls back inside from the door of Sulbha's office, where three girls are seen coming in, headed by Mangala, who carries two cups of tea in her hands. Subhash sits resting an arm on his suitcase, which is on Sulbha's desk. He is talking to Sulbha, who sits on the desk, left of frame, and leans towards him, laughing. The camera moves left to show Mangala looking at them with undisguised curiosity.

SUBHASH: What can I do? I had so many cases.

MANGALA (*looking at Subhash*): Bai, tea——

SULBHA (*turning to her*): You give it to him.

MANGALA (*shyly coming forward and handing Subhash a cup*): *Namaste*, Sahab.

SUBHASH (*smiling*): *Namaste.*

SULBHA: This is our Mangala. A very clever girl.

OTHER GIRLS: *Namaste Sahab!*

SUBHASH: Really? (*They both take a sip of the tea.*)

SULBHA: It's not very tasty, is it?

SUBHASH: No, it's fine. What else can you expect here?

Subhash takes out a cigarette. In the background a crowd of girls can be seen at the door. Sulbha bends forward and touches his shoulder as she speaks.

SULBHA: Subhash! You haven't given it up yet? (*She quickly withdraws her hand as the girls start giggling.*)

SUBHASH: Hmm? Er, where are your living quarters?

SULBHA: Come, I'll show you. (*They rise.*) Will you go round the Ashram first?

SUBHASH: No, I have had enough of it while coming in. I can see the rest tomorrow. Let's go. (*They start walking towards the door.*)

View from outside the office. Sulbha and Subhash come out of the room, followed by a crowd of girls. Some girls stand outside the room, they greet Subhash as they come out.

SULBHA: Girls, why don't you go away?

Undeterred, the girls continue to follow them till Sulbha finally manages to send them away.

> SULBHA: Why are you coming after us? Sahab will be staying here for four or five days now. Go on, go back to your work! (*The girls reluctantly give up following them.*)
>
> SUBHASH: Really! They are making me feel like a film star! (*They move away to the right.*)

The passage and the outer door of Sulbha's quarters, seen from the bedroom. A three-legged stool stands to the right of the bedroom door. Sulbha and Subhash enter the passage.

> SULBHA (*as they come to the bedroom*): Come in. This is my palace. Had I known you were coming, I would have tidied it up a bit.
>
> SUBHASH: No, no. It'll do. It is unimportant where you stay. I have not come here to admire the scenic beauty! (*He sits on the stool. It tilts backwards. Subhash saves himself from falling over by putting his arms against the wall. Sulbha grabs hold of him at the same time with a startled gasp. They both laugh. He rises, holding her hands.*) How thin you have become!

Suddenly looking more purposive, he pulls the curtain across the door, and draws Sulbha towards the filing cabinet on the right, on which she has kept the photographs. He holds her close and caresses her passionately.

> SULBHA: Subhash! Subhash!

There is a knock on the outside door. When it is repeated, Sulbha frees herself and moves away to the left. Subhash stands feeling frustrated, leaning against the cabinet. He sighs impatiently and rubs his face with his hands.

Three girls stand in the passage. Sulbha comes from the right.

> SULBHA: What's the matter?
>
> ONE GIRL: What kind of food will the Sahab have?

Subhash still stands near the cabinet, looking thwarted.

> SULBHA (*off*): Subhash!

The girls and Sulbha. The girls smile expectantly and whisper among themselves.

SULBHA (*calling out to Subhash*): The girls want to know what kind of food you would like to have.

Subhash rests an arm on the cabinet.

SUBHASH: Under the present conditions, anything prepared with clean hands will do.

Sulbha sends the girls off, casts a worried glance towards the inner room, then walks towards it.

SULBHA (*to the girls*): The usual food we have every day. (*They leave.*)

Sulbha moves aside the curtain to appear at the door of the bedroom. She looks at Subhash, who is out of the frame, on the right. She walks into the room. Camera pans with her to where Subhash stands leaning close to the cabinet, sulking.

SULBHA: Subhash! They are so happy to see you here. They were waiting eagerly to see my husband.

SUBHASH: Are they satisfied now, or is there something left still?

SULBHA: Why are you behaving like this? You know what unfortunate lives these girls have, how deprived they are.

SUBHASH: But why should that bother me?

SULBHA (*reproachful*): Subhash!

SUBHASH: Sorry. (*He rises and moves to the right, the camera following him. Sulbha is out of the frame.*) Sulu, I admit that I don't have the same kind of understanding of social problems as you have. But I don't interfere with other people's lives; and the least I expect is that they should not interfere with mine. (*He sits down on the bed. Sulbha comes into the frame from the left and places her hands affectionately on his shoulders.*) But I do sympathize with other people's sorrows! (*He smiles, and with a sigh, gives up the argument, taking her hands in his own.*) Sulu, I always feel as if somebody is watching us here. (*She giggles.*) Hey, what makes you laugh? I'm telling you, there are eyes behind each door and window. Shall I suggest something? We have the car. Let's go out somewhere. Come on.

SULBHA (*smiling*): Yes, let's.

SUBHASH: But you'd better get out of those school-marmish clothes.

6

SULBHA: Why, Subhash! (*They laugh. She moves away to the left, followed by Subhash.*)

Subhash and Sulbha sit among tall grass in a field. The car can be seen parked a little way behind. Far away on the horizon, a line of hills. The camera draws closer. Sulbha has her head tilted back, her eyes closed. Subhash looks around carefully, chewing a blade of grass. He looks at Sulbha and touches her face lovingly with the blade of grass. She laughs and bends her head. He smiles and, putting an arm around her, draws her closer for a kiss. A loud noise of a bicycle bell is heard and they move apart guiltily.

In the distance a cyclist goes across the field, not looking at them at all.

Sulbha and Subhash sit together as before, but the precious moment is lost. They laugh ruefully together. Sulbha looks at her watch, and gasps.

SUBHASH: What's the matter?

SULBHA: Subhash, let's go.

SUBHASH: Why?

SULBHA: It's six o'clock! Time for the meals at the Ashram. (*Subhash looks disappointed.*)

SUBHASH (*reluctantly*): Come on. (*But neither of them gets up.*)

SULBHA: Come on!

SUBHASH (*looking innocent, repeats Sulbha's words*): Come on! (*They smile at each other and rise.*)

Dusk is falling by the time the car turns into the gates of the Ashram. View through the windshield of the car. In the fading light, near the open veranda on the left stands a *tonga*. Satyabhamabai and another girl hold on to Mangala, who is in great pain. Others stand watching. The car stops.

SATYABHAMABAI: There, see! Bai has come.

The car, from the point of view of the girls. Subhash sits at the wheel. Sulbha rushes out of the car.

SULBHA: Mangala, what's the matter? (*Mangala groans with pain.*)

SATYABHAMABAI: She's been having a lot of pain.

SULBHA (*affectionately to Mangala*): Does it pain very much?

MANGALA: Oh, Bai. I'm so scared! Please don't leave me alone!

SULBHA: No, I won't leave you. (*Subhash comes and stands by the tonga.*) Subhash! Will you take us to the hospital? I may have to wait there for a while. But you can come back.

SUBHASH (*reluctantly*): All right.

He moves away to the right. Camera follows the small group around Mangala, taking her to the car.

SULBHA: Come—be careful. (*To Mangala*) You have to bear it for a while.

The car with Mangala and Satyabhama sitting in the back seat. Camera moves to show Subhash going round the bonnet towards the driver's seat.

SULBHA: We'll reach there in five minutes. Bai, hold her carefully. Let's go.

The camera pulls back to show Sulbha near the passenger door. She stops and exchanges glances with Subhash, who stands on the other side of the car. Subhash looks annoyed; Sulbha, pleading and helpless. Then they both get into the car in silence. Subhash reverses the car.

A close view of Mangala's face bathed in sweat. She is in great pain.

A corner of the veranda in the hospital. A doctor approaches the camera, which draws back to reveal Sulbha waiting on a wooden bench on the right, resting her forehead on her hand. She rises with a start when the doctor addresses her.

DOCTOR: Mrs Mahajan.

SULBHA: What is it, Doctor?

DOCTOR: A normal delivery will not be possible. She may need a Caesarean. But the girl is very weak. It'll be better if you call her relatives here.

SULBHA: I've already sent an attendant. But they won't be able to get here so soon.

DOCTOR: The operation cannot be delayed. Will you sign the form then, as her guardian?

SULBHA: Yes, I will.

DOCTOR: Right. I'll send the form with the Sister. (*He goes back the way he came. Sulbha moves towards the camera, her head bowed in thought. She stops and turns to the right.*)

A close view of the lamp in the operation theatre.

Gloved hands attach a blade to a scalpel.

A doctor and his assistant in their robes, caps and masks.

Sulbha paces up and down the length of the veranda, looking worried.

A room in the hospital. The doctor and his assistant come in by the door on the left, followed by a nurse. Camera pulls back to show Mangala lying on the bed, moaning, a thin pipe inserted into her nose. One of the doctors checks her blood pressure. Sulbha sits on a stool by the side of the bed, wiping the sweat from Mangala's forehead with the end of her sari.

> SULBHA: Calm down.
> MANGALA (*groaning*): Oh, don't do that, sir! Oh!
> ONE OF THE DOCTORS: What is she saying?
> SULBHA: Her teacher—had taken her by force.
> DOCTOR: That's terrible! Er, Mrs Mahajan, she bled profusely. And it is difficult to match her blood group in this small town. Anyway, let us try. (*To the other doctor*) Dr Kulkarni—— (*They go out of the room, talking, followed by the nurse. Sulbha turns to Mangala.*)

A close view of Mangala; she is tossing and turning, her eyes rolling over.

A close view of Sulbha watching anxiously.

Mangala on the bed, moaning and breathing with an effort. Sulbha sits beside her, gently wiping her forehead.

A close view of Sulbha looking scared, pressing her fingers on her lips as she watches Mangala, who is out of the frame.

A close view of Mangala, who is visibly sinking, gasping for breath.

A close view of Sulbha, whose face reflects the growing understanding of what is to come.

Mangala takes a last laboured breath, then falls completely silent.

Sulbha removes the fingers from her lips slowly, trying to reconcile herself to what has happened.

Night. A top shot of the Ashram gate seen from the courtyard inside. The gatekeeper opens the gate. Sulbha enters, still in a state of shock. The gatekeeper shuts the gate as she walks slowly into the courtyard. On the sound-track, the song sung at the prayer meeting.

> *Song*: This our sacred home is a reflection of your presence.
> In the wind and the stars I have read your name.
> All creation, birth and death,
> Are expressions of you, O compassionate one.

With the song still on the sound-track, Sulbha walks towards the camera from the left, as it pulls back slowly.

Sulbha enters the passage of her quarters, shuts the door behind her and leans against it, all the time looking at the floor. She leans her head back against the door, takes a deep breath and looks towards the bedroom.

Sulbha's view of the bed where Subhash lies asleep, his hand on an open book, the table lamp spreading its dull glow in the room.

Sulbha near the outer door as before. She gulps, trying to hold back her tears, then moves towards the camera.

Sulbha stands just outside the bedroom door. She sobs aloud once, then quickly covers her mouth with her hands. The camera moves with her as she goes towards the bed, tears running down her face at last. She sits down slowly on the bed, then falls on Subhash's chest, weeping uncontrollably. Subhash wakes up with a start, lifts her ravaged face and stares at her.

> SUBHASH: Sulbha! Uh! What's the matter? Sulu, Sulu, what is it? What's wrong?
> SULBHA (*crying helplessly*): Don't ask me anything now, please!
> SUBHASH (*holding her, letting her cry*): Calm down. Hmm?

The gatekeeper beats the gong twice, marking the hour of the night.

Sulbha and Subhash lie on the bed in the dark. Subhash, who is awake, turns to Sulbha, straightens her, putting her on her back, then leans over her.

SUBHASH (*desiring her*) : Sulu!

SULBHA (*still tortured by her experience*) : Subhash, please, not now.

Subhash turns away, upset by her rebuff, and lies back on the bed beside her, with an arm under his head. Sulbha, wide awake now, stares at the ceiling silently, unable to react.

Morning. Outside Sulbha's quarters, a close view of Subhash, who shuts the boot of the car. Camera draws back swiftly to reveal Sulbha at the stairs on the left, carrying his suitcase. She comes forward.

SULBHA: Give Rani my love, to Maya, Bhauji* and mother-in-law also——

SUBHASH: All right. (*He takes the suitcase from her without a smile, and gets into the car, pulling the door shut abruptly.*)

SULBHA: And look after yourself! (*He does not look at her, but starts the car and waves casually.*)

SUBHASH: Bye. (*The car moves away. The camera pans with it going towards the gate. Some girls stand watching. Kamlabai walks towards Sulbha, who is out of the frame on the left.*)

Sulbha turns to go into her quarters, when Kamlabai calls her, coming into the frame from the right.

KAMLABAI: Bai, wasn't the Sahab going to stay for a few days?

SULBHA: Hmm? Some urgent work came up suddenly and he had to leave. (*She goes into her quarters, leaving Kamlabai staring after her.*)

Jangam and another girl escort a bride and a groom, decked with flowers, out of a room in the Ashram. Camera pulls back outside the door where a row of girls stand on either side, with Sulbha on the right, turned away from the camera. The bride and groom hold flowers in their hands. They both bend to touch Sulbha's feet. Sulbha protests.

SULBHA: What is this? (*She pulls them up gently.*)

The groom stands on the left. Sulbha has her arms on the bride's shoulders as she stands facing her.

*Brother-in-law.

SULBHA: Susheela, I've done all this on my own responsibility, without taking the permission of the Committee. Be happy. Don't make another mistake. (*Turning to the groom.*) And you too, take care of yourself, and make her forget about her old days.

GROOM: Yes, Bai.

The gatekeeper sits near the open gate, watching, and stroking his moustache thoughtfully.

Sulbha gives a new sari to Susheela as a parting gift. They all smile as the bride and groom walk down the stairs towards the camera. Jangam and Sunanda follow, as the camera closes in on Sulbha's face.

SULBHA: Look after yourselves.

Sulbha looks at her album in her room. The pages turn, showing Sulbha and Subhash in their happiest moments, the growing Rani and the love they shower on her. In between' shots of the turning pages of the album come the colourful memories of happy days spent on the beach, in the sun. A series of dissolves show Rani growing from a chubby baby to a happy child. On the sound-track a song is heard.

> *Song*: In this empty hall of music
> I sing your song.
> It is a night of emotions.
> It is a night of the full moon.
> I don't know whom I seek,
> I don't know whose face it is.
> But over and over again,
> It is your smile that I see in the mirror.
> My friend, it is your song that I send you.
> There it stands in your garden,
> A silent Parijat tree.

Sulbha shuts the album. The camera closes in on her eyes, brimming with tears.

Mrs Samson strides across the courtyard angrily, with Sulbha following her, trying to reason with her. The camera moves with them, showing the girls of the Ashram in the background, engaged in different activities.

MRS SAMSON: I don't like it at all! It is all very irregular!

SULBHA: I have some idea of its being irregular, Madam. But this was her chance of a new life. And I felt that it was within my authority to help her to achieve it.

MRS SAMSON: Don't tell me anything!

Sulbha and Mrs Samson walk towards the camera as it pulls back.

MRS SAMSON: But she was married once before!

SULBHA: That's technically correct, but, Madam, her husband is impotent. (*They stop and face each other in front of the camera.*)

MRS SAMSON (*shouting*): Whatever it is! It is still wrong of her to go away with another man when her husband is alive. (*She starts walking towards the right, followed by Sulbha.*)

SULBHA: But she has left on her own responsibility. And the man she has gone with is her old sweetheart.

Mrs Samson marches ahead of Sulbha down the courtyard. She turns to Sulbha near the gate, where the gatekeeper can be seen in the background.

MRS SAMSON (*shouting*): If anything goes wrong, the Ashram's image will be spoilt. This is a public institution. We must avoid complications. (*She stops and turns to Sulbha.*) And look, you are not to take any important decision yourself.

SULBHA: But, Madam, surely the Ashram is not more important than the women who stay here.

MRS SAMSON: Oh yes? It looks like the Committee must take some drastic action about it.

She turns away sharply, and gets into the jeep as the camera draws back, and the gatekeeper, giving her a big salute, runs after the jeep to shut the gate. Sulbha moves away to the right thoughtfully.

A section of the courtyard of the Ashram. Sulbha approaches the camera slowly, as her voice is heard over the sound-track, composing a letter to Subhash.

SULBHA'S VOICE: Dear Subhash, it is many days since you came here. I have written at least five or six letters to you. But I have not received a single letter from any of you. Do you know that just now there are five girls here taking a teachers' training course, and seven girls are training to be nurses? Subhash, all that I had wanted to do, all that for which I came here—I think at last those dreams of mine are taking shape. Oh yes, Subhash, the girls want to celebrate the *Chaitragauri** festival now. There'll be a lot of merrymaking.

A small makeshift stage or platform with a red backdrop, decorated with silver paper and flowers. Two little goddesses stand on the platform, their hands raised in blessing. At their feet trays of fruits and flowers, and a brass lamp glowing in the middle. Sunanda's song begins while the girls gather around Sulbha and Kamlabai. Kamlabai welcomes Sulbha in the traditional manner, offering her gifts of copra and grain.

A group of girls dance to Sunanda's song. A series of shots record the celebration. Jangam's eyes follow Sunanda as she sings. Sunanda smiles back at Jangam. The girls pull Sulbha into the dance. The dance carries on in front of the stage carrying the goddesses, as Sulbha moves away with a happy smile.

> *Song*: The moon is wild tonight,
>   How do I restrain it?
>   My body is on fire tonight,
>   How do I hold it back?
>   The full moon spreads its intoxicating light,
>   Blinding me,
>   Taking away my reason.
>   The sea rises in a fury of colours,
>   And the waves explode in a wild dance.

A length of open veranda at night. A door opens with a creak, on the right. A girl comes out in the shaft of light from the open door. She gestures to someone inside and walks away from the camera in the dark. A small group of girls follow the first one out of the room.

Sugandha's face appears next to a wall. She gestures to the girls behind her, then turns the corner and goes left, followed by Shobha, Champa, Jaswandi, Farida and others.

View from the top. In the light of the gas lamp the girls are seen walking towards the peon and the gatekeeper who join them.

*A festival marking the beginning of the new year by the Hindu calendar, when married women are felicitated.

The peon flashes his torch at the camera as the group moves to the left in the darkness, camera moving with them.

A winding iron staircase seen in the light of the torch.

A view from the top, of the peon coming up the stairs carrying his torch, followed by the others.

An opening in the terrace wall. Sugandha, the peon, the gatekeeper, and some of the other girls, appear at the head of the stairs and look around furtively.

In one corner of the terrace, Jangam holds Sunanda in a loving embrace. They sit huddled together on the floor of the terrace, Jangam caressing Sunanda.

Sugandha comes into the terrace, followed by the other girls, all of them looking accusing and curious at the same time.

Jangam turns and notices the girls, who are out of the frame. Her expression of gentle affection changes to one of fear. She releases Sunanda and sits back. Sunanda, who has her back to the camera, turns around looking scared.

The girls on the terrace look grim and accusing.

Jangam and Sunanda rise to their feet. Sunanda adjusts her clothes and only then turns around to face the crowd.

The girls march down the terrace to the left. They stop and start abusing Jangam and Sunanda, who are out of the frame.

GIRLS: Over-ripe fruits, shame on you! What sort of behaviour is this? (*A girl spits at them.*) Let's go! (*They rush to the left, the camera moving with them, as they reach the two girls. Jangam and Sunanda are indiscernible in the crowd which drags them forward, shouting and abusing them all the time.*)

Hearing the noise, Sulbha comes out of her quarters, tying her hair in a knot. Camera pans with her to show the crowd of girls bringing Jangam and Sunanda. They come and stop in front of Sulbha.

JASWANDI: They must be taught a lesson! They should be thrown out of the Ashram!

SULBHA: Let go! (*The girls are still holding on to their captives.*)

Sulbha faces the camera. Two of the girls are partially visible in the foreground.

SULBHA: Let them go! What have they done?

Some of the girls seen over Sulbha's shoulder. Jangam stands with her head lowered, next to Sugandha.

SUGANDHA: That which they should not do! It's been going on for a long time. Today they were caught at it.

A close view of Sulbha, right of the frame, looking towards the left.

Sunanda's face left of the frame. She lowers her eyes.

A close view of Sulbha as before. She frowns.

Jangam's face left of the frame. She looks up, pathetic and guilty, then lowers her eyes.

Sulbha's face left of the frame, looking at the girls.

Jaswandi stands next to Sunanda, with a section of the crowd.

JASWANDI: We have been keeping an eye on them. And a little while ago we found both their beds empty!

A close view of Sugandha, left of the frame, looking angry.

SUGANDHA: They were up to their tricks in the terrace in the dark— doing that which a man and a woman do together.

Some of the girls seen in the foreground, with their backs to the camera. Facing them stands Sulbha. She is joined by Kamlabai, looking worried.

Bakula among the girls, looking vicious.

BAKULA: You should give them a good thrashing!

Shobha makes her comment.

SHOBHA: We don't want them here!

Gulab speaks up from from the crowd.

GULAB: They should be ashamed of themselves! What kind of women are they?

Sulbha stands facing the girls, some of whom can be seen in the foreground. Kamlabai and Rukminibai stand next to Sulbha.

SULBHA: Stop it! I will look into the matter. Go back to your barracks, all of you. I said, go back! (*The girls leave reluctantly, grumbling among themselves. Sulbha turns to Jangam and Sunanda.*) Do you have anything to say?

Jangam and Sunanda face the camera. They stand silently, with their heads lowered.

Sulbha, Kamlabai and Rukminibai seen standing in front of Jangam and Sunanda, who have their backs to the camera.

SULBHA: Hmm. Bring them to the office. (*Kamlabai and Rukminibai come forward and take the girls away to the right.*)

Another view of Sulbha, who turns left and goes towards her quarters.

Day. Tirodkar's office and press. Sulbha walks towards the camera from the left. Camera pans as she reaches Tirodkar's desk. She is carrying a newspaper in her hand.

TIRODKAR: What an extraordinary surprise! What brings you here? Sit down, please do!

SULBHA (*throwing the newspaper on his table*): Have you seen this?

TIRODKAR: What should I get you? Tea? A cold drink?

SULBHA: Have you seen this piece? An exposure of lesbianism in the Ashram?

TIRODKAR: Oh yes, the one about illegal relations between people of the same sex!

SULBHA: Yes.

TIRODKAR: It is we who published it. (*He pretends to go back to work.*)

SULBHA (*sitting down*): You are a member of the Managing Committee of the Ashram, aren't you?

TIRODKAR: Yes, I am.

SULBHA: Well, then?

TIRODKAR: So what?

SULBHA: And still you can print such a piece about the Ashram?

TIRODKAR: Certainly! It is my duty as a journalist. We must print the truth about ourselves as well.

SULBHA: Yes, but you could have consulted me before publishing it!

TIRODKAR: Yes, but then how would it be a scoop? That's where the fun lies. (*Sulbha gets up and leaves.*) What? Are you leaving?

A procession of girls, talking excitedly among themselves, walks past the camera, to the left.

GIRLS: Today we'll get a final decision.

A mirror image of Sulbha, putting a *bindi** on her forehead. Camera draws back to show her in front of the mirror, adjusting her clothes.

Camera moves up to the girls marching past the camera.

A close view of Sulbha having tea. Camera pulls back to show her bending over her books and files, reading and marking something in a book as she sips her tea. She closes the book and looks out through the window.

Camera pans to the left as the procession of girls goes past the corner of a building, the girls talking among themselves.

GIRLS: We don't want girls like them here!

Sulbha bolts her door from outside. Sound of the girls approaching. She turns towards the noise. Camera moves to show her coming down the stairs on to the courtyard as the procession reaches her.

GIRLS: Come on, tell her. You tell her!

SULBHA: What's the matter?

SUGANDHA: We have to tell you something.

SULBHA: Come to my office.

SUGANDHA: No. We shall tell you here.

*Vermilion, a sign of marriage.

Sulbha seen over Sugandha's shoulder.

SULBHA: What is it?

A closer view of Sulbha with her back to the camera. Sugandha and the girls stand facing her.

SUGANDHA: We don't want those two girls in the Ashram.

Sulbha seen over Sugandha's shoulder.

SULBHA (*sternly*): Why?

Sugandha in front of the group of girls. One of the girls speaks up from the back of the group.

GIRL: Because they are bad girls. They are immoral.

Bakula stands between Jaswandi and Sugandha, a little behind.

BAKULA: Either they leave, or we do.

A close view of Sulbha.

SULBHA: Who has decided that?

Sulbha faces the girls.

GIRLS: We have decided.

A section of the girls with their backs to the camera in the foreground. Sulbha can be seen facing them on the other side.

SULBHA: Who runs this Ashram?

Jaswandi and Sugandha with the other girls.

SUGANDHA: That does not matter. This is our . . .

Rukminibai and Satyabhamabai, who have joined Sulbha, exchange glances.

SUGANDHA (*off*): . . . final word.

A close view of Sulbha.

SULBHA: Don't you know what people outside say about you? According to them you are all bad girls, all immoral!

A section of the group with Bakula.

BAKULA: And do they allow us to stay with them?

A close view of Sulbha as before.

SULBHA: So you won't allow those two to stay with you either!

Sulbha stands facing the girls in front of her quarters.

GIRLS: No, no. We won't!

A close view of Sulbha.

SULBHA: Then where will they go?

Gulab seen between Jaswandi and Sugandha.

GULAB: Anywhere! Let them go and die!

A close view of Sulbha.

SULBHA: And if I keep them here, where will you go?

Disconcerted, the girls look at one another.

The girls in the foreground, with their backs to the camera. Sulbha stands facing them.

SULBHA: They too have nowhere else to go. I shall decide later what is to be done about them. But they will stay here. (*She moves away to the left.*)

GIRLS (*as they disperse in different directions*): Come on, we'll go to the Chairmanbai.

A close view of Mrs Samson left of the frame. Camera draws back as she speaks. A large, bound volume lies on her lap, and she turns the pages as she talks to Sulbha, who sits right of the frame.

MRS SAMSON (*looking at her book*): They must go! I don't want to hear anything more. Send them to another Ashram.

SULBHA: Hmm. But their going away won't solve the problem. All the girls of the Ashram are guilty of some offence or the other. Where will you find someone who is completely free of guilt and has nothing but good in him? Madam, I assure you, these girls will definitely improve with psychiatric treatment.

MRS SAMSON (*looking up from her book with a frown*): I can think of other alternatives, but not this. They must go. (*She goes back to her book.*)

A close view of Sulbha, still trying to persuade Mrs Samson.

SULBHA: A doctor or a nurse would not react to a disease in this way. To them a disease would be a disease, whether it is of the mind, or the body. But we——

A close view of Mrs Samson, looking outraged.

MRS SAMSON: What are you defending, Mrs Mahajan? A woman like you, who comes from a respectable family?

A close view of Sulbha as before.

SULBHA: I am not defending anything, Madam. I am just trying to ascertain what my role should be.

Mrs Samson and Sulbha in Mrs Samson's drawing room.

SULBHA: And I feel that——
MRS SAMSON (*ignoring Sulbha*): Shekhar! Take the Bai in the jeep to the Ashram. (*The audience is over. She goes back to her book.*)

Sulbha sits in shocked silence, then rises, moving towards the right, the camera moving with her. She stops near a huge potted plant to say good-bye to Mrs Samson, who is now out of the frame and does not respond.

SULBHA: Thank you, Madam. (*She goes right.*)

Night. The Ashram gate viewed from outside. In the dark, two girls sneak out of the wicket gate, and pull it shut behind them. They look through the peephole into the Ashram before walking cautiously away to the left.

The Ashram wall seen from outside. The two girls—Bakula and Gulab—look around them carefully, then run left to a scooter-rickshaw, which is just starting up. The girls get into the scooter-rickshaw, which leaves in a hurry.

Night. Sulbha's office. Sulbha sits at her desk to the right of the frame. The peon, the gatekeeper, and Rukminibai are standing near the desk. Sulbha is talking to the police over the telephone.

SULBHA: Hmm. Both of them are wearing saris that are worn in the Ashram. They are from the slums of Bombay. All right. You send Constable Zagre, I'll keep the photographs ready. What?

VOICE (*off*): We know who must've kidnapped the girls. A nasty, big rich man from here around. They'll be back soon.

A close view of Sulbha, right of the frame, listening to the voice over the telephone. Her face registers shock and embarrassment. She hastily replaces the receiver on the cradle, looks at those in front of her as if to check up whether they could possibly have overheard the conversation.

SULBHA: You may go.

Day. Hot *dal** being poured onto plates from a large vessel. Camera pulls back to show Sugandha distributing *dal* to a row of girls on a veranda. Behind her, Jaswandi is distributing something else to the other row of girls, sitting against the wall of the rooms, and facing the first row. A hum of conversation is heard.

A closer view of some of the girls having their meal. The conversations that can be heard clearly amidst the general noise include comments on the food being served as well as the method of serving.

The two rows of girls having their meal. Sugandha, Jaswandi, and another woman advance towards the camera as they serve the food to the girls.

Jangam, who has her back to the camera, looks up at Sunanda in the opposite row. Sunanda returns the look.

From over Sunanda's shoulder, Jangam is seen looking at her. She lowers her eyes after a while.

Two girls in Sunanda's row whisper and giggle together.

Sugandha and Jaswandi, who have been serving the food, are now closer to the camera. They both rise and exchange glances, then look towards Jangam, who is out of the frame.

*Split pulse cooked in gravy.

7

Their view of Jangam eating with the others.

Sugandha and Jaswandi continue their work, leaning away from the camera on either side.

A close view of Mukta and Farida giggling together.

Jangam in the foreground left. Sugandha pours *dal* on the plate of a girl sitting near her, and gives Jangam another look.

Two girls sit against the wall, eating their food.

In the foreground, Jangam, with her back to the camera. Sugandha bends in front of her with the vessel of hot *dal*.

Jangam in the foreground on the left. Next to her sit Mukta and Farida. Sugandha in the foreground, hesitates, then pours the hot *dal* on Jangam's arm. Jangam shrieks with pain. Everybody turns to her.

SUGANDHA: It was accidentally spilt!

The other row of girls. Girls start rising and running to the scene of the accident. Camera turns to show Jangam shrieking with pain. Jaswandi rushes up to her and they all crowd around.

SUGANDHA: Really! It was an accident. (*Everybody talks at the same time.*)

A close view of Sunanda still sitting where she was, watching Jangam, who is out of the frame.

One woman strokes Jangam's head to console her. Sugandha dabs at the burnt arm with a duster. Jangam snatches her arm away, shrieking.

Girls crowd around Jangam, who cannot be seen. Jaswandi hands her serving bowl to one of the girls and runs down the length of the veranda to the right, camera moving parallel to her.

The crowd of girls out of focus in the foreground. Sunanda passes behind them, looking towards the camera, tearfully. Camera follows

her to the left as she reaches a wooden pillar at the edge of
the veranda, and weeps, holding on to it.

Camera follows Sulbha and the attendants running down the
veranda to Jangam.

SUGANDHA: Bai has come. Now tell her what you want to say.

JANGAM: She burnt me purposely!

SUGANDHA: Why should I do that? Do I have any quarrel with
you? Huh?

SULBHA (*pulling Jangam up and handing her to Satyabhamabai*): Bai,
take her to the hospital at once. Take a rickshaw. I'll follow.

SUGANDHA: If I am in the wrong . . . (*Sulbha turns towards the girls.*)

Girls stand in the foreground with their backs to the camera. Sulbha
turns to look at them. She is fuming with rage.

SUGANDHA: . . . I'm ready to take my punishment.

SULBHA: Sugandha, you have been carrying on a personal war
against Hirwe and Jangam. I've had my suspicions. And
Jaswandi, who is a very clever girl, has been supporting you.

Sugandha and Jaswandi in front of a group of girls, facing the camera.
Jaswandi looks at Sugandha, then turns to Sulbha, who is out of
the frame.

JASWANDI: Why are you blaming me, Bai! What . . .

A close view of Sulbha in a rage.

JASWANDI (*off*): . . . have I done?

SULBHA (*in a grim, low voice*): Admit your offence, Sugandha.

A close view of Sugandha, looking sulky.

SUGANDHA: It was an accident.

Farida and Mukta in the foreground. Sulbha looks left, in a state of
suppressed violence. Camera moves with her as she admonishes the
girls, finally turning to Sugandha again.

SULBHA: It was not an accident. You have done it purposely.
Jaswandi and you have planned it between you. And all these
girls have seen what happened. But they will not speak out.

Because you boss over them and will create trouble for them.
They are all scared of you.

Camera moves across the girls, who all try to look innocent, except
Sugandha, who is still looking defiant.

SUGANDHA: No, Bai. That is not correct.

Sulbha near Sugandha and Farida, in a close view, looking towards
Sugandha as she speaks.

SULBHA: Girls who live in this Ashram must obey only the orders of
the Superintendent. I shall put an end to all bossing around.
(*She turns and walks to the right.*) As a punishment, Jaswandi and
Sugandha will wash all the vessels today. (*She stops near a pillar.*)
And no one is to help them. Understand? (*She turns and walks
to the right.*)

At the well, Sugandha and Jaswandi wash huge cooking vessels,
scrubbing them clean.

Sulbha walks past the barracks with the peon. Rukminibai and the
tailoring teacher walk behind her. She hands her files to the peon,
looks at the watch as she walks, and stops near the gate when she
hears the gatekeeper shouting. Bakula and Gulab are seen coming in,
escorted by two policemen. The girls wear printed nylon saris, one
blue, the other pink. The policemen salute Sulbha, stopping a little
beyond the the gatehouse. The camera follows Sulbha as she walks
up to the girls, who stand looking defiant.

POLICEMEN: Come on, you bitches! (*To Sulbha*) *Salaam*, Baisaheb.

The girls stand with their backs to the camera in the foreground, with
Sulbha facing them. The tailoring teacher and the peon are seen
behind her on either side.

SULBHA: What did you gain by running away?

A close view of Bakula, who screams viciously at Sulbha.

BAKULA: We ran away because we don't want to stay here!
What do we stand to gain by staying here? (*She spits at Sulbha
noisily.*)

A close view of Sulbha, who refuses to react. She turns to the other girl, who is out of the frame.

SULBHA: What have you got to say?

Gulab in a close up, looking equally vicious.

GULAB: He said, we could go to Delhi, we could go to Bombay!

A view of the whole scene. The policemen on the left, the girls facing Sulbha, and the peon, Rukminibai and the tailoring teacher behind her.

SULBHA: Put them in the lock-up. (*To the policemen*) You can go. (*They leave, saluting her. The tailoring teacher and Rukminibai drag the girls away to the right, the girls resisting all the way.*)

BAKULA AND GULAB: Let go! We don't want to stay here! Let go, or we'll run away again!

Girls stand in clusters, watching Bakula and Gulab being dragged through the courtyard. They stop as they are going past the well, where Sugandha and Jaswandi are washing clothes and vessels.

Sugandha and Jaswandi look at the runaways.

Gulab struggles to release herself from the tailoring teacher's grip.

Jaswandi looks at Bakula and Gulab, who are out of the frame.

Bakula struggles with Rukminibai as she looks at Jaswandi and Sugandha, who are out of the frame.

A close view of Sugandha frowning at the runaways.

They are all seen together. Bakula and Gulab are dragged away to the right, watched by Sugandha and Jaswandi. Camera follows their course round the side of the well.

A close view of Gulab biting her nails nervously. Camera pulls away from her as she pushes back her hair from her forehead and turns to look at the path outside the window. Sulbha can be seen on the path in the distance.

GULAB: Bakula, come here, quickly! (*Bakula joins her at the window.*)

A closer view of Gulab and Bakula on either side of the window, looking out grimly. They turn to each other, then turn back to watching Sulbha, who is out of the frame.

The open door of the lock-up from the inside. The tailoring teacher and Rukminibai walk in, carrying plates of food for the girls.

RUKMINIBAI: Come on, take your lunch!

The girls stand at the window. They turn round sharply at Rukminibai's call, looking resentful. In the distance, Sulbha can be seen walking down the path leading to the lock-up.

View from outside the window. Bakula and Gulab turn to look outside the window again. Rukminibai and the tailoring teacher are visible in the background.

Inside the room the camera draws back from the girls as they turn away from the window again, to face the attendant and the teacher. Sulbha is still seen on the path behind. She is nearer the window of the lock-up. The girls leave the window, defiantly advance into the room. Gulab knocks the plate out of the teacher's hand. It falls with a clatter on the floor.

Sulbha approaches the camera looking towards the lock-up, which is not in the frame. What she sees, startles her. She quickens her pace, moving to the right.

The attendent and the tailoring teacher giving the girls a thorough beating. Their shouts and the girls' screams fill the room.

Overpowered by the superior strength of the older women, Bakula and Gulab lie on the floor while the attendant and the teacher pound away at them.

A close view of Gulab held by the hair, her head being dashed against the floor.

Sulbha runs up to the window in the foreground.

SULBHA: Bakula! What is happening here? (*She rushes to the right, camera following her movement as she runs in by the door at the side of the room.*) Rukminibai! Don't beat the girls! Stop! Stop hitting them!

Nobody hears her in all the noise. Gulab's face is seen distorted with pain as her head is knocked on the ground.

SULBHA (*off*): I say, stop it!

Gulab lies in the foreground, pinned down by the tailoring teacher. Beside her lies Bakula with the attendant hitting her. Sulbha rushes in to push Rukminibai away from Bakula. The tailoring teacher rises.

SULBHA: What kind of uncivilized behaviour is this! Didn't I ask you to stop it? (*The girls still crouch on the floor. Sulbha pulls Bakula by the arm. Bakula jerks it away with a shout, looks up and realizes that it is Sulbha, and rises slowly.*) Clean up all this mess! (*Camera draws closer to her.*) And get them fresh plates of food!

BAKULA (*now out of the frame*): We don't want to have food here! We won't even take water here! We'll not stay here!

Camera on Sulbha alone, who gives a warning glance to all of them and moves away.

A film show in the Ashram. The girls can be seen in the dark, sitting on the floor with their backs to the camera. On the screen a dramatic sequence with blazing guns and car chases.* A series of shots follow. In the half-light, Sulbha is seen sitting next to the projectionist's table, on a chair. She rises and moves away to the right.

The lock-up window seen on the right of the frame. Screams are heard inside. The gatekeeper is seen rushing up to the window. He takes one look and starts shouting.

GATEKEEPER: Hey! The girls are burning! (*He runs helplessly back to the window again.*)

Inside the lock-up, Bakula and Gulab are rushing around the room, their clothes on fire.

*Kasme Wade, 1980

View from inside the lock-up. A small gap in the wire netting on the window. The gatekeeper tries to pull the netting apart, but fails. The girls' screams rend the air. The gatekeeper looks horrified.

Inside the lock-up, Gulab falls on the floor in a heap, burning.

The gatekeeper struggles with the netting on the window desperately. The girls are heard screaming inside.

Outside the lock-up, the gatekeeper leaves the window and moves to the locked door next to it, shaking the door and tugging at the lock.

GATEKEEPER: Roll on the floor, girls!

A view of the girls inside the lock-up, rolling on the floor, the flames rising from their bodies. They scream.

The gatekeeper tries to pull apart the gap in the netting.

His view of one of the girls on fire, rolling on the floor.

The gatekeeper puts his shoulder against the door in an effort to break it open.

One of the girls near the lock-up wall, on the floor, burning. Flames rise in the foreground from the other girl.

The gatekeeper pushes at the door, which refuses to yield.

GATEKEEPER: The girls are on fire!

One of the girls lies on the floor on her stomach, flames rising from her back. She lifts her disfigured face towards the camera, then drops it, screaming.

The gatekeeper moves from the door to the window again.

GATEKEEPER: Roll on the floor!

One of the girls lies on the floor, screaming.

The gatekeeper stands with his back to the camera, pushing the door in an effort to open it. In the dark, Satyabhamabai and the tailoring teacher rush up to him with blankets.

GATEKEEPER: The girls are burning! Tell the Baisaheb! Where are the keys?

SATYABHAMABAI: With the Bai. (*She drops the blankets and runs back into the darkness.*)

GATEKEEPER: Get me a stone!

TAILORING TEACHER (*picking up a stone*): Take this.

Another view of the girls burning helplessly on the floor.

Sulbha reclines on the bed, with her back to the camera. Rukminibai rushes into the room.

RUKMINIBAI: Bai, Bai! Come quickly! Gulab and Bakula are on fire!

SULBHA: What!

RUKMINIBAI: Yes. (*Sulbha rises from the bed and runs out ahead of Rukminibai.*)

At the film show. The audience are sitting with their backs to the camera. The projector is seen on the left. Satyabhamabai appears from the right, and whispers the bad news to the girls, who rise and rush away to the right.

A close view of the gatekeeper still struggling with the lock, trying to break it with the stone.

One of the girls inside the lock-up lifts her head from where she lies burning.

Girls run out of the film show, leaving the room empty.

In the courtyard outside, a crowd of girls rushing away. Sulbha joins them from the right.

Sulbha in the foreground, followed by the inmates of the Ashram and the peon, run towards the left of the camera.

One of the girls in the lock-up lifts her head as she lies on the floor.

View from inside the lock-up. The door has finally been opened. The gatekeeper, Satyabhamabai and the tailoring teacher rush in with blankets, and wrap them around the writhing girls, beating the flames out.

In the dark, the peon and the crowd of girls run towards the camera.

Sulbha runs into the lock-up. She shrieks, covers her eyes and reels back. Kamlabai holds her from behind as Sulbha extends her arm across the door to stop anyone else from entering. She approaches the now still bodies slowly, with horror, and tears in her eyes. Camera tilts down as she kneels by the side of the girls. Sulbha touches the foreheads of the girls. Kamlabai sits and cries, covering her mouth.

> SULBHA: Quiet, now! Bakula, why did you do this? (*She holds Satyabhamabai's arm.*) Listen, I am going to ring up for the ambulance. You stay here, all right? (*She rises and goes out, making her way through the crowd.*) Come, make way. (*She goes out of the room. The crowd closes in again.*)

Sulbha walks past the outer wall of the Ashram, holding on to the wall with one hand. She comes close to the camera, which pans to show her leaning her head against the wall. She sobs, then covers her mouth as nausea overcomes her. She turns her back to the wall, takes a deep breath, looks around with frightened eyes, then starts walking again, towards the right.

The Managing Committee in session. As usual Mrs Samson sits at the head of the table. But the seat next to her, where Sulbha used to sit, is empty. Camera faces her from the other end of the table, and closes in on her slowly as she speaks.

> MRS SAMSON: Members, some of the more important charges against our Ashram Superintendent, Mrs Mahajan, are: her total responsibility for the death of two girls who committed suicide by burning themselves in the lock-up. This event was discussed in the Legislative Assembly and unfavourable comments were made about the Ashram. Aiding and abetting a girl to marry another man when her husband is still alive and, in the process, giving a bad name to the Ashram's activities. Being rude to the honourable MLA over the telephone and using impolite language. Spoiling relations with traders who have been on good

terms with the Ashram. And stubbornly experimenting with new ideas in the name of modernization.

Tirodkar and Vadimbe in their usual seats. Biscuits and tea in front of them.

TIRODKAR: Excellent. Absolutely correct and to the point.

VADIMBE: No, no, discipline is a must. (*He raises his cup of tea to his lips.*)

A close view of Sheila Samson. She looks around the table as she speaks.

MRS SAMSON: This morning I got a call from the Secretariat in Bombay. To enquire into all these events, the government has appointed a one-man commission. The enquiry will begin in a day or two.

View from inside Sulbha's bedroom. Sulbha is seen entering the room, taking out the pins from her hair. She looks greatly upset, almost in a state of shock. She stops near the steel cupboard on the left, then starts walking slowly again, deep in thought. Camera moves with her till she rests the pillow against the head of the bed, and sits against it, slowly leaning back, frowning. On the sound-track Sulbha's voice is heard, composing a letter to her husband. Camera draws closer to her face till she is in a big close up.

SULBHA'S VOICE: Dear Subhash, I received your letter. You have asked whether you can help in any way. What should not have happened, has happened. But I have faith in my own sincerity. Don't worry about me. Sulbha.

Night. Sulbha sits at her desk in the office, in the light of the lamp, holding her clasped hands near her mouth. She frowns as she stares in front of her. The telephone rings, she picks it up. It is a man's voice.

VOICE ON THE PHONE: Bai, it is not good for a woman like you to stay alone in a small town. There are men here who don't just think evil, they are evil. (*Sulbha replaces the receiver on the cradle.*)

Another view of Sulbha staring in front of her. The telephone rings again. She lifts the receiver. It is a man's voice again.

VOICE ON THE PHONE: Is it Mrs Mahajan? How many girls are you going to kill in the Ashram? Aren't you satisfied yet? Eh? (*She puts the receiver back on the cradle.*)

Sulbha in the foreground with her back to the camera. The peon enters and hands her a long, fat envelope.

PEON: Chairmanbai has sent this. (*He turns to go, then turns back to Sulbha again.*) You are going to make your rounds, aren't you, Bai? (*Sulbha nods. The peon salutes and leaves. Sulbha opens and reads the letter.*)

On the right of the frame, a close view of Sulbha reading the letter. She holds the paper closer, purses her lips and reads on grimly. She puts the paper down as the phone rings. She turns to the telephone and picks the receiver up.

SULBHA: Hullo.

Bane sits on his divan with an expensive shawl round his shoulders, and the politician's white cap on his head. An antique metal horse stands in place of the wood carving, behind the glass lamp. Bane leans on a bolster as he speaks.

BANE: *Ram Ram.* This is the MLA, Bane. What has been happening in that Ashram of yours, eh? Here I have to answer for you in the Assembly. Have you seen the newspapers of Pune and Bombay? Then what have you decided? You should pack your bags and leave. There are many unsavoury characters in this town. For want of a better solution, they may even burn the Ashram. They'll certainly come to the Ashram. If you are not there, at least the Ashram will be saved. So . . .

A close view of Sulbha on the right of the frame, listening to Bane.

BANE (*off*): . . . what have you decided? Huh? (*Sulbha replaces the receiver grimly, rises, and moves away to the left.*)

A close view of the gatekeeper, right of the frame.

GATEKEEPER (*shouts*): Everything is a—ll right! A—ll right!

The gas lamp near the outer wall. The gatekeeper walks away from the camera, knocking his stick on the ground.

The courtyard in front of Sulbha's office. Sulbha comes out of the office, stops and looks around, then moves away to the left.

From a distance, Sulbha is seen walking towards the camera. She walks past a veranda, moving away to the left.

The path past the outer wall. From a distance, Sulbha is seen walking down the path towards the camera, the wall on her left. Suddenly, a shower of stones fall on the path from outside, some hitting Sulbha, who tries to cover her head with her arms. The gas lamp goes off, its glass covering shattered by the stones.

A close view of Sulbha in the dark, covering her head with her hands. She lifts her head, removes her hands, and looks towards the right. A cut is revealed on the left of her forehead, bleeding a little. She touches it, then looks at her blood-stained hand. She turns again to the right, looking scared.

Sulbha stands in the dark, right of the frame. She hears footsteps rushing away outside. She starts walking towards the camera, and moves away to the left.

The one-man commission. A big close up of a fat, baby-faced man with a cigarette, condescending and aloof. Camera draws back as he speaks.

> MAN: Now tell me, what made you leave your home and family, and take up the job of the Superintendent here? Did you have any personal problems? If you find this question too personal, ignore it.

A close view of Sulbha, right of the frame. She frowns, then clears her throat and begins talking.

> SULBHA: I have a happy family life, and there was no financial need either. But I had no definite role in the family. I felt that I was idling away my time. And when the opportunity came . . .

Another man sits writing down Sulbha's statement.

> SULBHA (*off*): . . . I took it up as a challenge.

A close view of Sulbha as before.

SULBHA: On the one hand I had a degree in social work. On the other hand, basically, I had a sympathetic interest in women who are social outcasts, their lives, their problems. I felt I could relate to this sort of work.

A view of all three at a table. The man who is making the enquiry sits on the left of the table, facing Sulbha, who sits on the other side. The clerk writing down Sulbha's statement sits facing the camera.

MAN: Hmm. When you joined this place, did you find it very different from what you had imagined it to be?

Camera over the man's shoulder, looking at Sulbha. It draws closer to her as she speaks.

SULBHA: Yes. I had never imagined that an institution like this would be run in such an unsatisfactory manner. This institution was being used by a certain class of people for their own purposes. You may not be aware—or maybe you are aware—that this institution was providing girls to some well-known personalities outside. (*She stops, waiting for some reaction.*)

All three in the frame as before.

MAN (*expressionless*): Go on, I'm listening.

A close view of Sulbha. The camera draws back as she speaks.

SULBHA: I decided to change all this. But while making my efforts I realized that it was impossible to change anything here. Because the world of the Ashram has a deep-rooted relationship with the wider world outside, which is completely beyond my control. (*The camera moves left, behind the man, keeping Sulbha in view.*) Take, for example, the Managing Committee of this Ashram, the world outside that these women have known, the various people in authority who can exercise their power on this Ashram; for all these people . . .

A big close up of the one-man commission, right of the frame, smoking. He seems completely untouched by Sulbha's intensity.

SULBHA (*off*): . . . it was desirable that this Ashram should remain a prison.

A closer view of Sulbha. On the left foreground the clerk can be seen. Camera moves to the right as she speaks, behind the man making the enquiry, and closes in on her face, till she is on the left of the frame, and the mark on her forehead can be seen, where the stone had hit her.

SULBHA: Those who have no place outside are thrown in here. Those who become a problem for the people outside are locked up here. Those activities that cannot take place outside must take place here. As if such institutions are the dustbins of the established society outside. And when the bins start filling up and the filth overflows, the women are thrown out somewhere else, without any consideration for their feelings. Clear out the garbage for your own convenience, and then forget it! And this is what they call rehabilitation! (*Sulbha looks up for some reaction and is surprised by what she sees.*) You're listening, aren't you?

Over Sulbha's shoulder, the man can be seen sitting with his eyes shut, resting his head on his hand. He opens his eyes with a mild start, and smiles reassuringly. The camera moves left, to a closer view of the man.

MAN: Do I look like a judge? I am giving you all my attention. Go on, speak.

Sulbha's face in profile, right of the frame.

SULBHA: Gulab and Bakula wanted to escape from the confines of this dustbin into a freer world outside.

A big close up of the one-man commission, impassive, resting his chin on his hand as he listens to Sulbha.

SULBHA (*off*): They ran away the moment they got an opportunity.

A close view of Sulbha's profile right of the frame. She speaks with passion.

SULBHA: Do you know what Bakula said when they were caught and brought back? She said, what do we stand to gain by living here? She spat upon the life here. Gulab said that those people had told them they could go to Bombay, to Delhi. All they had known till then were the slums, filthy and nauseating. They wanted to live in a beautiful world. And we brought them back and put them in the dustbin again, and told them that they would have to stay here, like two-legged animals. In their eyes I was the destroyer of their dreams, their jailer! Their keeper! If it had been possible, they would have burnt me! They would have burnt this institution, these high walls! (*Threatened with tears, she shuts her eyes and covers her face with her hand, controls her emotions, and speaks in a low voice.*) But it was not possible. So they burnt themselves.

A close view of the man, who listens to her impassively.

Sulbha's face on the right of the frame. She removes her hand from her face, looks up and starts speaking again, getting angrier as she continues.

SULBHA: How many examples shall I give you? Who will these scavengers ever save? What flower can ever blossom in this refuse dump?

A close view of the man, looking superior and indifferent.

MAN: Mrs Mahajan, your words seem to imply that such institutions should not exist at all.

A close view of Sulbha looking angry.

SULBHA: The institutions should remain. But those who have made mistakes—and is there anyone who never makes a mistake?— should be given the opportunity to change themselves for the better. You are not giving them that opportunity when you take away their personal freedom.

A close view of the man smiling slightly, on the left of the frame.

MAN: Under the present circumstances, all this sounds very romantic.

Sulbha sits across the table, fighting a losing battle, but refusing to give up.

MAN (*off*): Don't you think so?

SULBHA: Then it's the 'present circumstances' that must be changed. I shall not accept defeat. I'll continue to make my efforts. If not here, then somewhere else. But I will not give up.

A view of the one-man commission. He remains unmoved to the last.

MAN: Thank you, Mrs Mahajan.

The door of the office in the foreground. Sulbha is seen in the distance, sitting at her desk, talking over the telephone in the light of the table lamp.

SULBHA: Hullo, please call Chairmanbai. She's gone to the club? Give her a message. I am Sulbha Mahajan speaking. Yes, the Ashram Superintendent. Tell her that I am leaving tomorrow morning, and that she'll get my resignation letter tomorrow. No, that's all. (*She replaces the receiver.*)

A close view of Sulbha's face. The camera draws closer as the whistle of a train is heard on the sound-track. Her eyes are full of tears, but she still looks determined.

View from the porch of Subhash's home. In the distance, Sulbha comes walking down the drive, carrying her suitcase. Camera pans as she turns right to the stairs. She looks around, then climbs the steps slowly.

View from inside the drawing room. Sulbha enters the room slowly, deep in thought. Camera pans to show a housemaid straightening up from a low table.

MAID: What is it? Whom do you want? (*Sulbha stops at her query, then looks towards the camera as Maya's voice is heard.*)
MAYA: Who is it? Sulbha! How did you come so suddenly?
SULBHA (*as Maya walks up to her*): Just like that. (*They smile at each other.*)
MAYA: How are you?
SULBHA: I'm all right.
MAYA (*to the maid*): Hey, Drupada, take the bag in.
SULBHA: And how are you? (*The maid picks up the suitcase, and Sulbha and Maya follow her to the door of the bedroom, facing the camera.*)
MAYA: I'm all right too. Come, let's go in.
SULBHA: Where is Rani?
MAYA: She must be playing outside. Come inside, do. (*They go into the room.*)

8

View from inside Sulbha's bedroom. Sulbha and Maya enter by the door on the left. The maid goes out from behind them. Sulbha looks around the room, then turns back to Maya.

MAYA: You rest here. I'll send you some tea.

SULBHA: Yes. (*The camera pans away from her to the various familiar objects in the room, the dressing table, the bed, the desk near the window. They are all there, but the room looks bare and lifeless.*)

Subhash's mother sits alone at the dining table, reading a newspaper, with a telephone next to her. Maya stands next to her, pouring tea. Nani looks up at Maya.

NANI: Who has come, Maya? (*She goes back to her reading without waiting for an answer.*) What's going on?

MAYA (*handing her a cup, hesitating*): Nani, Sulbha has come. (*Nani gives Maya a sharp look, then goes back to her newspaper.*)

NANI: Hmm. (*Maya picks up a cup and moves away to the right.*)

View from the porch of the house. Rani seen coming down the drive, going hop, skip and jump, as she recites a poem. Camera pans as she goes up the stairs.

The door of Sulbha's bedroom in the foreground. In the distance, Sulbha can be seen standing inside the room. Rani comes from the left, with her back to the camera, still reciting her poem. She stops in her tracks as she sees Sulbha, who turns to the child with a smile.

SULBHA: Rani!

A close view of Rani. She looks suspiciously at Sulbha, who is out of the frame.

SULBHA (*off*): Come here!

Sulbha smiles at her daughter. But the smile fades when there is no sign of recognition from Rani.

A close view of Rani's unyielding face. She scowls at her mother.

SULBHA (*off*): Come, darling!

Rani scowls at Sulbha.

A big close up of Sulbha, who looks hurt.

Another close view of Rani looking suspiciously at Sulbha.

Sulbha and Rani in the frame together. Sulbha takes a tentative step towards Rani.

SULBHA: Rani.

RANI (*stepping back*): Hey, Aunty! (*She avoids her mother and runs out of the room by the door opposite the camera, into the veranda outside. Sulbha stands staring after her. After a while she bows her head and turns away to the left.*)

A television set on a stool next to a door by which Maya drags an unwilling Rani into Sulbha's room.

MAYA: Crazy child! Don't you want to meet Mummy?

RANI: No, no!

MAYA: Come and see what she has brought for you.

RANI: Really? (*Camera moves to show Sulbha on the left, holding some books in her hands.*) Show me what you have brought! (*Rani goes up to Sulbha, smiling.*)

SULBHA (*kissing Rani*): I was in such a hurry when I came away. We'll go in the evening and get them for you, all right? (*Rani retreats immediately, frowning.*) Rani! (*The child runs out of the room.*)

MAYA (*going after Rani*): Rani! Please stop, my child! Listen to me. Don't run away like that, stop! (*Camera draws closer to Sulbha, who looks hurt, then lowers her head, goes to the desk and continues with her work.*)

Sulbha stands at the mirror, putting a *bindi* on her forehead. She stares at herself in the mirror as a song is heard on the sound-track. It is a continuation of the same song that was heard when she sat looking at her album in the Mahilashram, going over the memories of happier days. A series of shots follow, as Sulbha arranges flowers in a vase, dressed in a bright red sari. She drapes a garland round her hair and, turning her back to the camera, stands at the window, waiting.

> *Song*: My dreams are of little use.
> They do not tell me what you have done,
> Or where you have given away

The love that was in your heart.
In this empty hall of music
I sing your song.

As the last strains of the song fade away, Subhash is seen entering the
house. He comes into his bedroom smiling, a cardigan draped casually
round his neck. Camera pans with him as he comes and stands beside
Sulbha, near the dressing table.

SUBHASH (*taking off the cardigan and loosening his tie*): How are you, eh?
Vahini rang me up to say that you have come.
SULBHA (*smiles*): Hmm. (*Takes off his tie.*)
SUBHASH: You'll stay for a few days, won't you?
SULBHA: Hmm. Do you drink nowadays? (*He turns his face away at
once, with an awkward smile.*)
SUBHASH: Occasionally. When there's a lot of strain, it relaxes me.
(*He takes off his shirt, hands it to Sulbha.*)
SULBHA: Won't you have your food?
SUBHASH: No, I've eaten. I'm not hungry. (*He goes away to the left.
Sulbha looks at the shirt and tie left in her arms.*)

Subhash comes out of the bathroom, towards the camera, after a
wash. Camera pans to show Sulbha with a towel which Subhash takes
and wipes his face with.

SUBHASH (*wiping his arms*): Did you meet Rani? (*He does not look
at her.*)
SULBHA: Yes. (*She helps him wipe his back.*)
SUBHASH: She's been ill.
SULBHA: Yes, Maya told me.
SUBHASH: How's your work going?
SULBHA (*quietly*): I gave it up. (*Subhash turns to her, looking surprised.*)
SUBHASH: Hmm? I don't understand.
SULBHA: I left my job.
SUBHASH (*he does not look pleased*): Why?
SULBHA: Not now. We'll talk about it later, all right?
SUBHASH (*hesitating, uncomfortable*): That means—you're not going
back? (*She leans against him, drawing his arm round her shoulder.*)
SULBHA (*with her eyes shut*): No. (*He holds her casually, looking dis-
turbed.*)
SUBHASH: Hmm. (*He turns to her at last, and holds her close.*)

Sulbha rests her head on Subhash's chest. She lifts her head to look at Subhash, who caresses her gently, then hides her face on Subhash's shoulder.

A close view of Rani, who is having a nightmare. Camera draws away from her to show her lying between Maya and Mohan. Rani moans and moves restlessly in her sleep. Maya wakes up and pushes Mohan awake.

MAYA: Hey! Listen! She has had a fright.

MOHAN (*turning on the lamp*): Rani!

MAYA: Look how she is sweating! No, no, there, there, child.

MOHAN: She had a bad dream. (*To the child.*) Go to sleep, my love, go to sleep. (*Rani calms down and turns to rest her leg on Maya. Mohan turns off the lamp.*)

Sulbha sleeps with her head on Subhash's chest, but Subhash lies awake. They have been making love. The light from the table lamp near the bed falls on Sulbha's bare shoulders.

SUBHASH: Sulu, are you listening?

SULBHA (*without opening her eyes*): Hmm.

SUBHASH: I wanted to tell you something. (*Hesitates*) When you—— (*Changes his mind.*) Oh yes, what happened about that one-man commission?

SULBHA (*opening her eyes*): They couldn't prove any of the charges against me. I sent in my resignation myself.

SUBHASH: Hmm. Listen. Certain events took place here while you were away.

SULBHA: It doesn't matter.

SUBHASH: No, no. It's important that you should know about it. I was alone here. You had gone away. There was no point in thinking about you. The need was entirely from my side. (*Sulbha starts listening to him curiously, frowning slightly. He hesitates, stroking her arm in an absent-minded caress.*) A—a woman came into my life. I mean, nothing serious. Nothing—I mean—emotional. Just a fulfilment of my needs. If you like, I can tell you all about it. Sulu, I can understand your needs. I hope you will understand mine. You are an intelligent woman. (*The camera draws closer to Sulbha's face. She starts moving away from Subhash.*)

A close view of Sulbha lying on her back on the bed. She stares blankly to the left.

> SUBHASH (*off*): Now you have come back. But I cannot sever this relationship. It is impossible.

A close view of Subhash on the bed, looking at the ceiling as he speaks.

> SUBHASH: Sulu, that does not mean that the relationship between us has to be disturbed. You can go on staying here. We can—we can be just as we have been before.

A close view of Sulbha as before. She lies staring to the left, the muscles of her throat twitching as the pain wells up.

> SUBHASH (*off*): Only, you'll have to make a small compromise. I have done it already.

Subhash on the bed as before. He goes on more confidently.

> SUBHASH: And I am certain that you will be able to do it. (*He covers his eyes with his arm emotionally.*) There is no alternative.

Another view of Sulbha on the bed, looking towards the left, away from Subhash, who is out of the frame, her face slowly distorting with pain. She gasps finally, holding her sari near her throat in a convulsive grip. She turns to the left, her whole body curving inwards, as she cries out in almost physical pain. The camera draws away from her slowly as sobs rack her body.

Day. The camera draws back from a view of the trees in the garden outside, into the room where Subhash lies peacefully asleep. He stirs, yawns luxuriously, slips on his watch, turns and stretches his arm to the left of the bed. There is no one there. He looks, lifts his head to glance at the foot of the bed, turns right, and sits up frowning, picking up his shirt from the side of his pillow.

Sulbha stands near the cupboard. She has her suitcase open in front of her on a small table, and is putting her books into it. She turns back to the cupboard.

Subhash, frowning, starts putting on his shirt.

Sulbha near the cupboard. She brings out saris from the cupboard and puts them in the suitcase.

Subhash moves away from the bed. Camera pans with him till he reaches the suitcase. He stands facing Sulbha on the other side of the suitcase.

SUBHASH: What is this? Where are you going? (*Sulbha does not reply, but turns to the cupboard, takes out petticoats and puts them in the suitcase.*) Don't be crazy, you are not going anywhere! (*Sulbha takes out her blouses and puts them in the suitcase.*) Where do you want to go?

SULBHA: I don't know. (*She puts some more saris in the suitcase.*)

SUBHASH: Look, don't get into a new adventure. You'll only have to come back again. (*She turns to the cupboard.*) Listen to me, you'll get used to it. (*He starts throwing the clothes back into the cupboard. She does not resist, but stands quietly watching him as he shuts the lid of the suitcase and puts it back on the cupboard. He looks at his watch.*) They must all be waiting for tea. I'll get ready. You come along too. (*He goes confidently to the right. Sulbha stands as before, leaning against the open door of the cupboard, her arms folded, a determined expression on her face.*)

View through the window of Sulbha's room. The family in the garden, having tea. Nani sits with her back to the camera, Mohan on the right, and Maya facing the camera. Rani stands in the centre, throwing and catching a large ball as she sings a nursery rhyme. Subhash joins them from the left.

MAYA: Subhash, here's your tea. (*Subhash sits opposite his mother, with an empty chair on his left. Maya hands him a cup just as Rani finishes her song and Mohan laughs, clapping his hands.*)

MOHAN: She's learnt the whole poem by heart! The whole poem!

Camera draws back into the room as Rani begins the song all over again. Sulbha comes from the right and stands near the window, watching the family at tea. She moves back against the wall and turns to face the camera, thinking. Camera closes in on her face, ending in a big close up of her eyes, as the whistle of a train and the noise of its rushing wheels rise in the background.

The landscape rushing by. Camera pans to show Sulbha at the window, staring out of the train.

Sulbha on a wooden seat in the train, with her suitcase beside her. She closes her eyes, relaxing at last, then opens them again to look outside the window, the wind whipping her hair across her face.

The last verse of the prayer song in the Mahilashram is heard over the sound-track as the credits appear on Sulbha's face near the window, and the landscape outside. Sulbha looks happy and at peace as she moves closer to her unknown destination.

> *Song*: You are my liberator.
> My eyes are your lamps.
> The song in my throat is yours.
> I surrender all to you, my beloved.
> You are the creator, you are the humble one.